Canada Firsts

Canada firsts

RALPH NADER

NADIA MILLERON AND DUFF CONACHER

M&S

Canadian Cataloguing in Publication Data

Nader, Ralph
    Canada firsts

Includes bibliographical references.
ISBN 0-7710-6713-5

1. Canada—Civilization—Miscellanea.
2. World records. I. Milleron, Nadia. II. Conacher, Duff. III. Title.

FC95.N33 1992   971   C92-093531-1   F1021.N33 1992

Printed and bound in Canada

Published simultaneously in the United States by:

Center for Study of Responsive Law
P. O. Box 19367
Washington, DC 20036

McClelland & Stewart Inc.
The Canadian Publishers
481 University Avenue
Toronto, Ontario
M5G 2E9

Over 50% recycled paper
including 10% post
consumer fibre
Plus de 50 p. 100 de
papier recyclé dont 10 p.
100 de fibres post-
consommation.

M - Official mark of Environment Canada
M - Marque officielle d'Environnement Canada.

The creative achievements of Canadians are the substance
of this book and we acknowledge these with pleasure.
In addition, we thank the many Canadians who helped this
effort through their writings, interviews, and resources.
Finally, we thank Claire Nader for her persevering
editorial help through various stages of the book,
and Beverly Orr for her steadfast efforts in its
production.

Dedicated to Shafeek Nader who early appreciated the peoples of Canada and their accomplishments.

[Canadians are] the people who learned to live without the bold
accents of the natural ego-trippers of other lands.

MARSHALL McLUHAN (1967)

Americans should never underestimate the constant pressure on
Canada which the mere presence of the United States has
produced. We're different people from you and we're different
people because of you. . . . Living next to you is in
some ways like sleeping with an elephant. No matter how friendly
and even-tempered is the beast, if I can call it that, one is
affected by every twitch and grunt. . . . It should not therefore be
expected that this kind of nation, this Canada, should
project itself. . . . as a mirror image of the United States.

PRIME MINISTER PIERRE TRUDEAU (1969)

Contents

TRANSPORTATION

ENERGY

COMMUNICATION

MEDICINE

EDUCATION AND SOCIAL WELFARE

FOOD

ENVIRONMENT

SCIENCE

SAFETY

ARTS

BUSINESS

SPORT

Preface

This entertaining compendium offers a series of quick flashes which, taken together, begin to form a picture of that elusive Canadian Identity. It is ironic (but quintessentially Canadian) that the book is the brain-child of activist American Ralph Nader, who told me he hoped the book would become a horn-blowing manual for his self-effacing Canadian friends and an illustration to his fellow Americans of the distinctiveness of their neighbor to the north.

Firsts by Canadians that may not surprise people on either side of the world's longest undefended border include the snowmobile, the Canadarm on U.S. space shuttles, insulin, the Laser sailboat, the games of Trivial Pursuit, ice hockey, lacrosse (known to its Algonquian Indian inventors as *baggataway*) and, grab your hoop, basketball. A case can be made for the telephone too, Alexander Graham Bell having declared it was "conceived in Brantford, Ontario, and born in Boston."

Many other Canada firsts may come as a surprise. Henry Woodward of Toronto invented the electric light bulb, selling his share in the patent to Thomas Edison. Kerosene, or coal-oil as it was then called, was invented by Abraham Gesner of Halifax, Nova Scotia. The painter roller, Fuller brushes, and the formula for Pablum all were created by Canadians. One half of Superman, "a symbol of the strength and greatness of the United States, " according to *Time* magazine, was created by Joe Shuster of Toronto (American Jerome Siegel was co-creator).

The imaginations of the authors quite evidently have

been captured by some of the fundamental differences between American and Canadian societies, beginning with slavery, which was much less widespread and ended sooner in Canada. In contrast to the Revolutionary War fought by Americans to gain their freedom, Canadians achieved theirs through peaceful evolution following the British conquest. Canada's mixed economy, its social programs such as universal health care, its arts institutions such as the Canada Council jump out at you and begin to explain why Canadians may want to hang on to their distinctivenesses.

Another irony: *Canada Firsts* was turned down by four Canadian publishers before McClelland & Stewart Inc. picked it up. How typically Canadian!

PETER KOHL
Guelph, Ontario, Canada

Peter Kohl is a management
consultant, writer, and
environmentalist. In a previous
life, Kohl was a Canadian
newspaper publisher.

INTRODUCTION
by Ralph Nader

The immediate stimulus to this collection of Canada's "firsts" came from an exchange at a half-dozen gatherings which I attended across Canada in the mid-Eighties. The discussions came around to the subject of why Canadians were so self-effacing and unassertive in advancing their points of view and recalling their points of achievement in the past. I would ask the audience for examples of when Canada was first either in the world or in North America. Invariably, the list would start with the discovery of insulin, the games of hockey and basketball, the invention of the telephone, standard time, Superman, and Trivial Pursuit. But the list would begin to peter out at fifteen or twenty accomplishments, with the later additions bordering on the minor. No matter the composition of the audiences, whether university students and faculty or members of professional groups, the list was just about identical and as short. So many first achievements were excluded that I wondered whether Canadians were indeed first in the world in modesty.

      Self-deprecatory comments in Canada's self-critical literature reflect a cultural trait that shows less self-confidence than a country of Canada's stature should possess. I grew up in a small town in Connecticut that was replete with self-deprecation and lack of confidence in the community—quite in contrast to its productive history and remarkable natural surroundings. I came to see how such a collective disposition can destroy potential, drain the spirit, and contribute to the feeling that the grass is always greener on the other side of the fence. It undermined a sense of community that was not additionally burdened, as Canada's has been, by vast distances, a divided culture, and two languages.

On the occasion of Canada's one hundredth birthday, Minister of Finance Mitchell Sharp's thoughts were mindful of this trait: "As I see it," he said,

> It is the task of the rising generation of Canadians to create a new confidence and a new sense of cultural and civic identity in Canada. Unless we achieve some success on this front—and I believe we are beginning to do so—the very real attractions of the vigorous society to the south of us may attract too many of our able people. Then the human resources and skills required to shape and direct a complex industrial economy will simply not be available to us in Canada.

Sharp's concerns were economic. The questions of Prime Minister Lester Pearson in 1966 were more comprehensive:

> Whether we can live together in confidence and cohesion; with more faith and pride in ourselves and less self-doubt and hesitation; strong in the conviction that the destiny of Canada is to unite, not divide; sharing in cooperation, not in separation or in conflict; respecting our past and welcoming our future.

A few months later, however, Pearson placed the Canadian future in a confident perspective:

> As we enter our centennial year we are still a young nation, very much in the formative stages. Our national condition is still flexible enough that we can make almost anything we wish of our nation. No other country is in a better position than Canada to go ahead with the evolution of a national purpose devoted to all that is good and noble and excellent in the human spirit.

As a boy I spent many summers with my Canadian cousins in Toronto and the Ontario lake country. With some familiarity of Canada, I would return to school to find among my classmates a sizable ignorance about the neighbor to the north. I began to realize that Canada was one of the United States' best-kept secrets. Later, after visiting my brother and his friends at the University of Toronto's Hart House, I learned that Canada was also the United States' best-kept colony. The enormous economy and population south of its border, the large portion of the Canadian economy owned by absentee Yankee investors, and the cultural domination would give anybody a "superior inferiority complex," to use the phrase of Andrew Malcolm, author of *The Canadians*. "It's simple," Pat

Muelle, a moving-van operator told Malcolm. "You Americans are much more confident than we Canadians. You are taught that from birth. And so are we." Robert Fulford, a leading Canadian editor, put his finger on a consequence: "My generation of Canadians grew up believing that, if we were very good or very smart, or both, we would someday graduate from Canada."

Attitudes are said to be changing. Canadians, whether they be real-estate investors, "snowbirds" in Florida, or athletes in international competitions, are becoming more extroverted, more aggressive, surer of their identity and patrimony. But there is a concern that Canadians are part of an imitative culture where, in one Canadian's words, "the idea of orginality is to be first to copy Americans." And, new pressures on Canada from the south come with lure of the Free Trade Agreement, which went into effect January 1, 1989. When economic policies and the maintenance of valuable Canadian social services clash in order to meet the demands of U.S.-Canada homogenization, which country is likely to bend? Though the second largest nation in the world, Canada's population is 27 million and its economy one-tenth the size of the U.S. economy.

A new era is needed, one that beckons new levels of national self-confidence to protect what Canada has that is best, which will benefit the U.S., too. This collection is meant also for people in the United States. Americans have much to lose if Canadians lose their self-reliance and originality when outside political, economic, cultural, and psychological forces lead them toward an indentured, duplicative society. The historical examples in this book are testimony to the benefits of heterogeneity over a homogenization.

Such a benefit came home to me right after the publication of my book, *Unsafe at Any Speed*, in 1965. At that time, the U.S. news media were quite reluctant to report criticisms of cars by make and model, which the book did. It was difficult to interest television stations or networks in the issue of unsafe motor vehicles, or in my book. However, CBC's program "This Hour has Seven Days" was interested, and I made my North American television debut in Toronto with the program beamed into autoland (Detroit) from the Windsor station. The U.S. media then followed with extensive coverage. Even before the Canadian program, the first documentary on unsafely designed automobiles was authored by the National Film Board whose producers had consulted and interviewed me in some detail.

In subsequent years, time and time again in striving to improve consumer rights in the United States, my colleagues and I would make reference to a superior situation in Canada such as the provincial ombudsman, cheaper pharmaceutical prices, complete health-insurance coverage, and greater concern over acid rain. The credibility in the United States of a reference to Canada is higher than an analogy to any other country because of the belief that Canada is on the same democratic wavelength.

Canada, the United States, and many other nations are entering a period when narrow nationalisms in the West are being diminished by an internationalization of the global economy. Taken too far, this international dependence and interdependency can undermine seriously healthy national characteristics of self-reliance, diversity, and governments which are closer and more accountable to the people. In the United States, we call the latter "home rule." At this juncture of history, multinational corporations are opting for the global economy—often pushing their tax, labor, environment, consumer, and other deregulatory objectives by reducing justice standards of the leading nations toward the lowest common country denominator. A counterbalance is needed which reaps the fruits of international cooperation but leaves the roots diverse and locally controlled.

A few qualifications about this volume are in order. It is by no means a complete listing of firsts and foremosts in the world or North America. Canadians have broken world sports records; other Canadians have achieved front ranking in the arts and sciences. They are not included here because their achievements compared to others in the same field are not clearcut, or, as in sports, are very temporary.

We have tried to present major firsts and foremosts conceived in Canada or by a Canadian, even though the invention may have first been marketed in the United States or another country. There is a long history of Canadian inventors having to go abroad in order to produce and sell their inventions; some instances are noted in the text.

Finally, though there are achievements described in this book from almost every region of Canada, many of these were the accomplishments of white males. Our Canadian associate, Duff Conacher, made a special research effort to diminish this inequity but, as he informed us, "it was largely irresolvable in part because of how our history books describe the past." Moreover, he noted, the conditions and climate were such that members of other groups— women, first people, and other minorities, as well as the poor were prohibited or obstructed from participating in much of the work from whence the achievements sprung.

Canadian author Margaret Atwood has described the Canadian-U.S. border as the longest one-way mirror in the world when Canadians look at the United States. This book encourages the view that a two-way mirror is long overdue in order for Canadians to nurture a firm appreciation of the history of their own accomplishments and in order for the people of the United States to recognize the value of an independent-minded Canada to their own well-being.

Historical Achievements

THE CONTRIBUTIONS OF THE FIRST PEOPLES

This book celebrates the accomplishments of Canadians. We acknowledge that by this we mean, essentially, the accomplishments of European culture transplanted to North America. We recognize that the history of any country, era, or event, though often presented as an objective report of the facts, is often a story passed on from person to person on through the years. The distortions that can occur in the continual retelling of this story are innumerable and diverse. People disappear and reappear; times, dates, names and places change, and whole cultures are lost and found. One need only examine the recent discovery of women's history (or more appropriately "herstory"), of the history of blacks in Canada, and the ongoing struggle to preserve and to communicate to a wider audience the history of the aboriginal peoples to realize that numerous voices are silenced in any historical account. As noted in the introduction, the accomplishments of these cultures have largely been ignored in our documented history, and we are only recently becoming aware of our own limitations in realizing the unique accomplishments of the aboriginal peoples. Set out below are some of the recognized accomplishments of the cultures that preceded the Europeans in North America by at least 12,000 years and possibly as many as 25,000 years.

The First People entered North America across a land bridge between Alaska and Siberia in small hunting bands. They had already learned to survive in a harsh northern climate and to make exquisite flint and obsidian spear points that were as sharp as any of today's surgical knives. They lived by hunting giant creatures such as the wooly mammoth.

While the European colonists basically adapted their transported culture to American conditions, the First People created many cultures, based on the resources of a diverse and changing land. Evidence of the early development of one of these cultures is found at the L'Anse Amour Burial Site in southern Labrador. It is one of the oldest known burial mounds in the world, built some 7,000 years ago—2,000 years before the Egyptian pyramids.

By the time the Europeans arrived in the 16th century, the First Peoples occupied every major region of what is now Canada. They spoke fifty-three distinct languages, some as different from one another as English is from Chinese. They developed diverse social and political organizations, based on the food resources available in each region. The nomadic hunters and gatherers of the eastern forest and of the barren lands of the North tended to live in small bands of kinsmen. In contrast, the abundant salmon runs of the Northwest Coast supported the first large villages in Canada.

The Iroquoian farmers of the St. Lawrence region developed a complex federation, which predated Canada's by at least 500 years. The best known Confederacy is the League of Five Nations—the Mohawk, Cayuga, Onondoga, Oneida, and Seneca—which became the Six Nations when the Tuscarora joined in 1722. Fifty hereditary sachems, or peace chiefs, met once a year in the Great Council of the League to make new laws and settle common problems. The laws and decisions of the Confederacy, though unwritten, were passed on by word of mouth and recorded in wampum, arguably the world's oldest constitution, predating the American Constitution by at least 200 years.

The constitution sets out the structures of a matriarchal society based upon the image of a circle. In the Mohawk nation, for example, there are nine clans, as nine sections of the circle. For each clan there is a women's part and a men's part, and a clan mother and male chief, who is chosen by the clan mother and is chief for life unless he makes a serious mistake and then the clan mother has the authority to remove him from office. The clan mothers make up a women's council, and the male chiefs make up a men's council. The men's council make the decisions, all by consensus, but they are observed by the women's council and if one or another of the male chiefs is blocking the consensus process out of selfishness, it can lead to removal from office, or impeachment as it became known when adopted by the founding fathers of the U.S. constitution. These are just a few of the aspects of the Iroquois peoples' constitution.

The First Peoples also showed a genius in their adaptation to the varied ecological regions of Canada. The Inuit learned to survive in one of the most extreme climates on Earth. They developed the kayak to travel in the frigid northern waters. Propelled by a double-bladed paddle, this lightweight vessel of seal skins stretched over a frame of driftwood or rib bones has never been surpassed in its combination of speed, stability and lightness, not even by its descendents made of space-age plastics that are used today. Today, the Inuit are also known world-wide for their sculpture and printmaking.

The people of the Eastern Woodlands created the birchbark canoe to travel rivers and lakes and the toboggan and snowshoes to move in winter. Birchbark canoes were constructed by sewing birchbark over a cedar frame with thread made from white pine roots. Although canoes today are made with other materials such as aluminum and fibreglass, the design used by the Algonquian hunters has not been improved. Snowshoes had a wooden frame and an inside string made of rawhide. Taken up by 19th-century Canadians, snowshoeing and tobogganning became popular recreation sports that continues today.

The Iroquoian-speaking peoples of the Great Lakes region were Canada's first farmers. They grew maize (corn), squash and beans which added to the variety of the European diet (along with the potato of the more southerly first peoples). They also grew tobacco. The Iroquoians also invented the game of lacrosse (which they called *baggataway*).

The first people of the Northwest Coast are famous around the world for their wood-carving skills. The best-known examples of their art are the free-standing totem poles that stood in front of their houses, though they applied themselves with equal skill to treasure boxes and everyday items such as spoons and bowls.

The people of the Plains developed the tipi, a cone-shaped tent well-suited to their nomadic life. The tipi was made from animal skins pieced together and draped over a framework of poles, which were tied together at the top.

Much of the early explorations which fame attributes to

Jacques Cartier, Samuel de Champlain, Samuel Hearne and others could not have been accomplished without the help of the native peoples. If the native inhabitants of Stadacona (now Quebec City) had not shown Cartier's men how to make a tonic containing ascorbic acid from bark, they might have all perished of scurvy during the winter of 1535. New France would not have existed without the trading and trapping skills of the native people. The famous far-flung trading network of the Northwest Company, which stretched from Montreal to the Pacific Ocean and arguably formed the basis of Canada itself, would have been impossible without the birchbark canoe. The native peoples continued to play a still generally unacknowledged role in the economic and military affairs of the Americas until the early 19th century. By the mid-19th century, however, the Europeans coveted the native land for agriculture and the partnership of the fur trade dissolved into dependency, coercion and neglect.

The native peoples of Canada have come to realize that solutions imposed by outsiders cannot help them maintain their societies. Their political renaissance of the last twenty years has reasserted their will to survive and they are increasingly looking to find their own answers by turning back to their own cultural values and by regaining a measure of their former sovereignty. They are reviving traditional ceremonies, pursuing new economic and political strategies and regaining control of a wide range of institutions which govern their lives, such as courts, health clinics and schools.

FIRST SOCIAL CLUB IN NORTH AMERICA

In 1604-05, the settlers of New France had a miserable winter on Ile-Sainte-Croix. Without much fresh water and food thirty-five men died of scurvy. By the next winter, the settlers had moved to a new "Habitation", built from the dismantled buildings of Ile-Sainte-Croix, and nestled against the North Mountain at Port-Royal, in the Annapolis Basin. Here, in a fit of optimism, French explorer Samuel de Champlain (c.1570-1635) took the initiative to organize and establish the Ordre de Bon Temps (Order of Good Cheer), the first social club in North America. Many of the settlers were officers who were used to the diversions of the court of France and the Order was established to keep up their morale.

A competition was introduced into the Order to further the involvement of its members. Each man was made "Chief Steward" once each fortnight or so and was responsible for hunting the game, preparing the meal, and entertaining the rest of the members. Sometimes the chief of the Micmac tribe, Membertou, would attend the meal.

Each member would try to outdo those who had come before him, and the entertainment became quite elaborate. A good example is Marc Lescarbot's play, *Le Théâtre de Neptune en la Nouvelle-France* (The Theater of Neptune in New France) first performed on several small boats in November 1606 with a cast of eleven settlers.

QUEBEC CITY
The Only Existing Walled City in North America

Known for its Old World, European charm, Quebec City is the first city in North America to be placed on the United Nations Educational, Scientific, and Cultural Organization's (UNESCO's) World Heritage list, alongside such wonders as the Taj Mahal, and cities such as Cairo, Florence, Damascus, and Carthage. The list designates the city as belonging to all humanity and to be preserved as such. As part of the designation, the city is to give particular attention to maintaining itself in its original condition. UNESCO provides protection and financial assistance, if necessary, to prevent businesses or other development operations from destroying the character of the site. Quebec City, the oldest city in North America, was awarded World Heritage status on July 3, 1986 as part of a week-long celebration.

The city was founded in 1608 by Samuel de Champlain (c.1570-1635). With the erection of the first masonry palisades between 1701-13, the process began that was to make Quebec City the only walled city in North America, earning it the name "Gilbraltar of America." In 1763, the city became the capital of the Province of Quebec. The British continued to build the wall around the city. The now famous citadel was built between 1820-31, but by mid-century the whole fortification structure was out-of-date. Quebec City was in decline as a port and center of the timber trade as Montreal became the dominant port in Lower Canada. However, as the major center of French culture and the only walled city and seat of the only Francophone government on the continent, Quebec City was recognized as a site of historic significance. In 1875, Lord Dufferin, Governor General of Canada, persuaded the city to preserve the old fortifications that surrounded the city, and the conservation and restoration have continued to this day.

The city is built on the edge of a cliff and the Upper Town holds many of the religious structures and fortifications. Today the Lower Town is composed mainly of residential and commercial buildings. Both parts of the city are protected under the World Heritage designation.

COLLECTION OF VITAL STATISTICS

The collection of vital statistics began with the registration by Church authorities of weddings, baptisms, and burials. Canada is one of the few countries in the world with records that go back three centuries. Priests in New France made their first entries in 1610 and by 1621 a law had been passed that required the registration of marriages, births and deaths in Quebec.

The first official census in what is now Canada was taken in 1666 by Jean Talon, who was called the "Great Intendant" of New France. It reported the population of New France as 3,215 inhabitants, exclusive of native peoples: 2,034 men, 1,181 women, and 528 married couples. This was the first regular census of an area larger than a single city to be taken by a country in modern times. Before Talon, it had been more than one thousand years since the Romans used a regular census as a measure of tax resources and manpower for the military. Talon's first census listed details of age, sex, marital status and occupation.

Between 1664 and 1754, fifteen censuses were taken of New France and nine of Acadia. The second census, taken on July 17, 1673, showed a population of 6,705; in 1739, the census of Canada recorded a population of 42,701. New items were added to each census—crops, livestock, buildings, churches, grist mills, sawmills, firearms, and swords. The modern concept of a census, as a method of providing information about the structure of society, was born in this process. On April 2, 1871, the first census of the Dominion of Canada was taken, recording a population of 3,689,257, including 2,110,502 people of British origin and 1,082,940 people of French descent.

Under the Statistics Act of 1918, the Dominion Bureau of Statistics (DBS—called Statistics Canada since May 1, 1971) was established and the cooperation of the provinces was sought in registrations on standard forms supplied by DBS. Eight of the nine provinces entered the cooperative system in 1920. By 1926, Quebec had also adapted its long-standing system to the national system.

R EV. JOSIAH HENSON— THE ORIGINAL "UNCLE TOM"?

In *Uncle Tom's Cabin* (1852), American author Harriet Beecher Stowe showed the inhumanity of slavery. Josiah Henson (1789-1883), an enslaved black man in Kentucky who escaped with his family on the Underground Railroad to Upper Canada (now Ontario) on October 28, 1830, is reputed to be the original character on which Stowe based her novel.

Henson settled outside Dresden, Upper Canada, lived there the rest of his life and died a British subject. While in Canada Henson, as an ordained Methodist minister, became the pastor of a church and set up a settlement and the first vocational school, the British-American Institute, for runaway slaves. Funds contributed by anti-slavery supporters in the northern states and England, where Henson met with Queen Victoria three times on visits to solicit funds, helped purchase a 200-acre site for the institute and set up a sawmill, gristmill, blacksmith and carpentry shops where ex-slaves could be taught useful trades. Today, Henson's tulip wood cabin at Dresden is a museum and historic site.

S LAVERY ABOLISHED IN CANADA BEFORE THE UNITED STATES

Slavery in what is now Canada was first practised by native peoples of the Northwest Coast. The first European to practice slavery in Canada is believed to be Gaspar Corte-Real, who, in 1501, enslaved fifty native men and women in Newfoundland. Black slaves were introduced by the French as early as 1608, though the first black to be recorded as a slave in Canada was a Madagascan youth baptized Olivier Le Jeune in 1632. On November 13, 1705, slaves in New France were declared to be "moveable property." The right of Canadians to have and sell native peoples as slaves was upheld by Gilles Hocquart (1694-1783), then Intendant of New France, on May 29, 1733. By 1759, there were 3,604 registered slaves in Canada, of whom 1,132 were black. The French preferred the native people as slaves, finding them more docile, and the English were actually responsible for bringing most of the African slaves to Canada.

After the British defeated the French in 1759, slavery continued to flourish. In 1783, the practice of slavery in Canada expanded when American Loyalists fled the United States, bringing their slaves with them. Ten years later, in 1793, under the leadership of John Graves Simcoe, the first Lieutenant-Governor of Upper Canada (what is now Ontario), the Upper Canada Abolition Act was passed. It was the first recorded legislation against bondage in any part of the British Empire. It was, however, compromise legislation. On July 9th of that year, the importation of slaves was prohibited by the law, but slavery was not abolished completely; the status of slaves already in Canada was confirmed, and their owners were required only to feed and clothe them properly. The Act did require that any child born in Upper Canada of a slave mother would become free at the age of 25, and that no voluntary contract of service could extend for more than nine years.

Simcoe and others were disappointed with the law, however it did help to change public attitudes to slavery, and shift the plight of blacks in Canada towards freedom. On August 23, 1797, the last slave transaction in Canada occurred when Emmanuel Allan was sold at a public auction in Montreal. In Lower Canada there was no political initiative to end slavery, so the initiative fell to the courts, and especially to James Monk, Chief Justice of the Court of King's Bench in Montreal. In 1798, he declared that slavery did not exist in Lower Canada, and left it up to slave owners to prove him wrong. Some tried, but none succeeded. In the face of a hostile court system, runaway slaves could not be recaptured, and slavery became untenable in the province. By 1811, it was no longer practiced in Upper or Lower Canada. Slavery was abolished in the whole of the British Empire by the Emancipation Act, which passed in 1833 and took effect August 1, 1834.

On February 26, 1851, the Anti-Slavery Society of Canada was founded in Toronto. At this time, the "Underground Railroad" was helping fugitive slaves to safety in Canada, before the abolition of slavery in the United States. Anti-slavery activities were heating up in Canada and on January 17, 1861, a mass meeting took place in Montreal to protest the return of escaped slaves to the United States. Finally, in 1865, slavery was abolished in the United States.

MARY SHADD CARY— First Black Newspaperwoman in North America

Born in 1823 in Wilmington, Delaware, Mary Ann Camberton Shadd ended up in Canada and went on to become the first black newspaperwoman in North America. In 1833, the Shadds moved from Delaware, a slave state, to West Chester, Pennsylvania, where Mary was raised and could be educated in a Quaker boarding school. In 1851, in response to the Fugitive Slave Law passed by the U.S. Congress in 1850, Shadd left for Upper Canada, arriving in what is now Toronto. She moved on to Windsor where she lived and taught school for a couple of years. In March 1853, she and others in Windsor established the *Provincial Freeman* as an alternative weekly newspaper for blacks in Canada to Henry Bibb's *Voice of the Fugitive*. Rev. Samuel R. Ward was editor of the newspapers, though Shadd was the key figure to its operations, and the first black woman to establish and edit a newspaper in North America, and probably the first woman to do so in Canada.

A year passed between the first and second issue of the paper and its headquarters were shifted to Toronto in 1854. Mary and her sister Amelia edited the paper while it was in Toronto in 1854-55, before William P. Newman took over the editorship in 1855 and moved it to Chatham, Ontario. After May 1856, Shadd acted as one of the paper's three editors until it ceased publication in 1859. Mary returned to teaching after the demise of the paper, first in Chatham and then, after 1868, in the United States. She died in 1893 in Washington, D.C.

I NVENTION OF GREEN INK

The invention of green ink may not seem like a major innovation, but counterfeiters would tell you otherwise. Green ink, used for printing American currency since 1862, was invented by Thomas Sterry Hunt, while he was a chemistry professor at McGill University between 1862 and 1868. A native of Norwich, Connecticut, Hunt (1826-92) studied at Yale University, and then joined the Geological Survey of Canada in 1847 as a chemist and mineralogist. During his time in Canada, Hunt taught at Laval University from 1856 to 1868 and McGill. He left Canada in 1872 to accept the geology chair at the Massachusetts Institute of Technology. However, throughout his career, Hunt maintained close ties with Canada.

Hunt's invention also led to the nickname for American currency: "greenbacks". The green ink was prohibitive to forgery because it was immune to photographic imitation. In 1859, Hunt was elected a fellow of the Royal Society of London. He helped found the Royal Society of Canada in 1882 and he became its president in 1884.

I NDEPENDENCE WITHOUT REVOLUTION

The United States won its independence by revolution. Canada, on the other hand, achieved its independence by a different means, by a negotiated transfer of powers over time, by evolution rather than revolution. It was a less spectacular method than the American one, but in the end it has proven to be more influential. By demonstrating that revolution was not a necessary prerequisite to independence, the evolutionary method pioneered by Canada made possible a model for the peaceful decolonization of other subject societies.

The first major step on Canada's road to independence occurred in 1848 when, after several decades of agitation, two rebellions and a Royal commission, two colonies in British North America, the Province of Canada and Nova Scotia, were granted a reformed system of administration known as "responsible government". The basic principles of this reform were British in origin, and in 1848 it meant that all members of the cabinet had to be drawn from among the sitting members of the legislature, and that the cabinet could direct the administration only as long as it could sustain the support of a majority of the elected members of the legislature. When it lost its majority, it lost its mandate to govern. With the addition of organized political parties to provide stable majorities, this is the system of government in Canada today.

Canadian politicians did not invent the concept of responsible government, but they were largely responsible for working out the means by which the system could be applied in colonial situation, and overcoming the hesitation of British politicians. The Canadian experiment was a success, and responsible government was quickly extended to other white colonies in the empire.

The next major step took place on July 1, 1867, when the British North America Act came into effect and the Dominion of Canada was formed. The BNA Act (now called the Constitution Act, 1867) gave the Canadian Parliament almost sovereign powers, although it was still prohibited from dealing directly with other states, controlling immigration or commanding the Canadian armed forces. The Act also set out the distribution of powers between federal and provincial jurisdictions.

Complete sovereignty was achieved gradually over the next sixty years. During that period four more colonies (Australia, New Zealand, South Africa and Newfoundland) and Ireland were granted "Dominion status" in imitation of Canada. In 1931, by the Statute of Westminster, the British government acknowledged that the Dominions were no longer in any way subordinate to the British Parliament, but were sovereign nations. At Canada's request, Britain agreed to retain control of the BNA Act until such time as Canada could work out a satisfactory amending formula. This was not accomplished until fifty years later, when the federal government under Prime Minister Pierre Trudeau undertook a process to patriate the BNA Act. On December 2, 1981, when the British House of Commons approved a resolution by a vote of 246 to 24, to patriate the Act from Britain with an amending formula and a Charter of Rights.

In recent years the federal and provincial governments have been negotiating changes to the Canadian constitution which would affect areas such as the amending formula, the distribution of powers between jurisdictions and others.

STANDARD TIME

Standard time. It is something we all take for granted. When thinking about friends or relatives across the country or in another part of the world, we can make a simple calculation and figure out what time of day it is there. Are they eating lunch just as we are waking up, or are we eating supper just as they head off to bed? But not too long ago, just over 100 years ago, time was not standardized across the world. For each community in Canada and other countries, the correct time of day was established by designating noon as the time when the sun was directly overhead. This led to confusing time variations between towns, which were being brought closer and closer together by faster and faster means of travel, and made scheduling for railways very difficult. It took a Canadian, Sir Sandford Fleming (1827-1915, knighted in 1897), to conceive and implement a standard time system that was international in scope.

On February 8, 1879, Fleming was lecturing at the Canadian Institute for the Advancement of Scientific Knowledge in Toronto when he first made public his suggestion that the world should be divided into 24 equal time zones, with a standard time in each zone. He had developed his workable system after a considerable and lengthy exploration of the time keeping systems of many cultures.

Some critics of his plan denounced him as a Utopian and maintained that the concept of Standard Time was "contrary to the will of God." However, Fleming was a powerful promoter of his idea, and on November 18, 1883, all North American railway companies adopted his idea; the next year at a conference in Washington, D.C. twenty-five countries adopted his proposition. On January 1, 1885 Greenwich Mean Time (GMT) was established as the meridian of the system and over the next several years countries around the world adopted the system. Since December 1985, Coordinated Universal Time (CUT), a chronometrical service based on atomic clocks and established in Paris in 1972, has been the foundation of standard time. Canada occupies seven of the 24 time zones, second in number only to the former Soviet Union, which occupies nine.

FIRSTS FOR WOMEN IN LAW AND GOVERNMENT

Clara Brett Martin (1874-1923) - First woman lawyer in the British Empire

Born and raised in Toronto, Clara Brett Martin was an exceptionally bright student and graduated at age sixteen with an honors degree in mathematics from Trinity College. One year later she applied for admission as a student to the Law Society of Upper Canada. She was rejected on the grounds that the Society's regulations restricted admission to "persons" only. Women were not legally "persons" at that time in Canada and so Martin was considered ineligible to study law.

In response, Martin formally petitioned for admission as a student-at-law, and with the support of the Dominion Woman's Enfranchisement Association she campaigned and succeeded in having a bill passed by the Ontario legislature on April 14, 1892 which permitted the Law Society to admit women to study law, and permitted women to practice as solicitors but not barristers (they could take clients but not appear in court on their behalf). Sir Oliver Mowat, then premier and attorney-general of the province, supported the legislation as a compromise designed to appease the suffrage movement without giving them the right to vote.

The Law Society's response to the legislation was to declare it "inexpedient" to set out rules for the admission of women to study law. Martin continued her campaign to be admitted and persuaded Mowat to intervene on her behalf. As a result, she was finally admitted in 1893. After enduring ridicule from male classmates, teachers and the press during her student years, she graduated. Next, in 1895, Martin petitioned the Law Society to allow her to practice as a barrister. She gained wide public support in her campaign, and the Law Society finally changed its regulations in 1897, allowing Clara Brett Martin to become the first woman admitted to the profession of law in the British Empire. She died in 1923.

Emily Murphy—First woman judge in the British Empire

Born in 1868 near Cookstown, Ontario as Emily Ferguson, Murphy was raised and educated in Toronto. She and Arthur Murphy, a theology student, were married in 1887, and moved to Swan River, Manitoba in 1903, and then Edmonton, Alberta in 1907. Arthur was a travelling missionary during these years, and Emily worked as a journalist, headed up the Canadian Women's Press Club and was involved in other women's movement organizations.

On July 1,1916, in an Edmonton courtroom, Emily Murphy spent her first day as a judge, the first woman appointed to sit as a police magistrate in the British Empire. She remained active on the bench until 1931. At the beginning her right to sit as a judge was often challenged by lawyers, who argued that since, under a British common law decision handed down in 1876, women were to be regarded as persons in matters of pains and penalties, but not in matters of rights and privileges, she could not legally enjoy the privilege of an appointment as police magistrate. Hence no decision of her court could be binding. Murphy always listened politely to the protest, took note of it, and passed on to the next case. However, when the second woman judge in Alberta, Alice Jamieson of Calgary, was challenged on the same grounds by a lawyer who took his case all the way to the Supreme Court of Alberta, which upheld Jamieson's decision, Murphy decided that the question of a woman's personhood had to be clarified.

She began a campaign on a related issue, gaining admission for women into the Canadian Senate, which was also limited to "persons." After eight years of meeting in vain with representatives from two different federal governments, Murphy decided that action had to be taken through the courts. On March 14, 1928, with four other prominent Canadian women as interested parties, Henrietta Muir Edwards, Louise McKinney, Nellie McClung, and Dr. Irene Parlby, Murphy petitioned the Supreme Court of Canada to decide whether women were "persons." Henrietta Muir Edwards was very active in the National Council of Women, while McKinney, McClung and Parlby had all served in the Alberta legislature. Five weeks later the court rejected their argument, which had been presented by their counsel, Newton W. Rowell, and declared that in its opinion, Canadian women were not "persons." The women appealed to the

Judicial Committee of the Privy Council, the final court of appeal in the British Empire, and on October 18, 1929, the Privy Council overruled the Canadian Supreme Court's decision and gave women legal status as "persons."

In April 1943, Helen Kinnear was appointed Judge of Cayuga (Ontario) County Court, the first woman appointed as a county judge in the British Commonwealth (as it was now called). Born in Cayuga, Kinnear became a lawyer in 1920, practicing in Ontario until her appointment to the bench. In 1934, she was the first woman named King's Counsel, and the following year became the first woman lawyer to plead a case before the Supreme Court of Canada.

Firsts in provincial legislatures

In June 1917, Louise McKinney (1868-1931) became the first woman elected to a legislative assembly in the British Empire when she was elected to Alberta's provincial legislature. Born as Louise Crummy and raised in Frankville, Ontario, McKinney became a teacher and then moved to the United States to become an organizer of the Woman's Christian Temperance Union (WCTU). There she met James McKinney, also an active prohibitionist, and they married in 1894. The McKinneys returned to Canada in 1903 and were pioneer settlers in Claresholm, Alberta. She helped to organize the WCTU in that area and headed it for the next twenty years. The introduction of prohibition in Alberta in 1916 is said to have been much more important to McKinney than her election one year later on a prohibition platform as a representative of the Non-Partisan League. However, during her term in office from 1917 to 1921 she urged the government to enact more effective social welfare legislation.

In March, 1921 in British Columbia, another political first came about when Mary Ellen Smith was appointed as a member of the provincial cabinet, the first woman cabinet minister in the Western world. First elected in 1918, Smith served for the next ten years in the provincial legislature, and was responsible for legislation that improved working hours, set a minimum wage for women, and set up a pension for poor mothers with dependent children. She also served as chairperson of the British Columbia Liberal party until her death in 1933.

On December 13, 1949, Nancy Hodges, member of the Legislative Assembly of British Columbia, became the first woman to be named Speaker of a legislature in the British Commonwealth. First elected in 1941, after spending thirty years editing the "Women's Page" of the *Victoria Times* newspaper, Hodges was re-elected three times before being defeated in 1952. She was appointed to the Senate in 1953. Ontario also marked a political first when Pauline McGibbon was appointed lieutenant-governor (representative of the Queen) of the province in 1974. It was the first time a woman had been appointed lieutenant-governor in Canada.

WORLD'S LARGEST ORGANIZATION OF WOMEN

In 1889, the infant son of Adelaide Hoodless (born Adelaide Hunter, 1857-1910) died from drinking impure milk. From that point on, Hoodless devoted herself to women's causes, particularly to the betterment of women's education for motherhood and household management. Essentially conservative, Hoodless never supported the suffragette cause and instead campaigned for domestic science courses in the schools, and advised the provincial department of education on the subject. She was involved in the formation of the National Council of Women of Canada (NCWC), which was organized in 1893 by Lady Ishbel Marjoribanks Gordon, Countess of Aberdeen (Lady Aberdeen). Hoodless was also involved in the formation of the national YWCA in Canada in 1894, and became its first vice-president and a year later national president. Again with Lady Aberdeen, she assisted in setting up the Victorian Order of Nurses in 1897.

On February 19, 1897 at Stoney Creek, Ontario, Hoodless founded the first of what was to become the Federated Women's Institutes of Canada, aimed at promoting knowledge of home economics, especially in rural communities. The first institute formed as the result of a speech by Hoodless before the Farmer's Institute at Stoney Creek. In Winnipeg in 1919, Judge Emily Murphy, the first woman to become a police magistrate in the British Empire when she was appointed in 1916, organized the Federated Women's Institutes of Canada and served as its first president. The Women's

Institutes has become the largest world organization of women, with chapters in fifty countries, and it remains active in areas such as home economics, citizenship, agriculture, and industry.

T ERRY FOX AND STEVE FONYO

On April 12, 1980, Terry Fox (1958-81) of New Westminster, British Columbia, began his cross-country "Marathon of Hope" to raise money for cancer research. Fox had lost his right leg to cancer in 1977, but he resolved to run across Canada, with the blessing of the Canadian Cancer Society, on a fund-raising campaign. His goal was to raise one dollar for every Canadian. After extensive training, he set out from Cape Spear, Newfoundland and over the next five months he captivated the heart of the country.

Unfortunately, on September 1, 1980, Fox was forced to stop his run just east of Thunder Bay, Ontario when it was learned that cancer had spread to his lungs. He had run a total of 3,331 miles (5,373 kilometers) at a pace of nearly 24 miles (40 kilometers) per day. A nine-foot high statue of Fox at the Terry Fox Scenic Lookout marks the point at which he stopped his run. On September 7, a national telethon raised more than ten million dollars and not quite two weeks later, on September 19, Fox was invested as the youngest Companion of the Order of Canada. He reached his goal by raising a total of $24.7 million for cancer research.

Terry Fox died of cancer on June 28, 1981. His determination and courage inspire thousands to raise funds by running in the annual Terry Fox Run and inspired Steve Fonyo, who also lost a leg to cancer, to run across the country. Beginning in 1985, Fonyo retraced the steps of Fox, and continued right across the country. It took him fourteen months to complete his "Journey for Lives." He raised thirteen million dollars for cancer research.

S HARON WOOD

Born in 1957 in Halifax, Nova Scotia, Sharon Wood now lives in Canmore, Alberta and is a professional climber and mountaineering instructor. At 9:00 P.M. on Tuesday, May 20, 1986, two days after her twenty-ninth birthday, she became the first North American woman to reach the summit of Mount Everest, two months after the Canadian team began the climb. It was the culmination of an expedition that began four years earlier, when Jim Elzinga, a native of Calgary, and two others quit the first Canadian group to attempt to climb the mountain and began planning another attempt. The first Canadian expedition in 1982 reached the summit, but met with tragedy in the process, losing three Sherpa guides and Canadian climber Blair Griffiths to ice falls and avalanches in the early stages of the climb.

The expedition led by Elzinga was called Everest Light, and lived up to its name in comparison to the 1982 climb, which involved a sixteen-person team, a one million dollar budget, ten tons of equipment and supplies, and many porters. Everest Light consisted of a twelve-person team, a three-hundred-thousand-dollar budget, three tons of supplies, and no porters. The expedition followed a steeper and more difficult, but also safer, route than in 1982, climbing up the Chinese side on the mountain's western ridge. They spent the first seven weeks establishing six camps along the route, with the sixth about 2,000 feet below the summit. By that time, the strenuous nature of the work had exhausted all but four or five of the twelve climbers. It was decided that Wood and Dwayne Congdon, also of Canmore, Alberta, would make a first attempt, and that Barry Blanchard and Albi Sole would make a second attempt, if possible.

Congdon and Wood began the climb from the base camp on May 14. They stayed overnight at the first camp and then spent the next day climbing to the second camp at 19,500 feet. The next three days were spent following a fixed rope to the sixth camp. On May 18, team members from the camps below sang *Happy Birthday* to Wood through their walkie-talkies. Congdon and Wood got an early start on May 20, waking at 5:00 A.M., but they took four hours to break camp and get moving because of fatigue. Twelve hours later, after facing fifty mile-per-hour (eighty kilometers) winds, and slowly ascending steep faces of ice and snow, Congdon and Wood climbed the last few feet to the 29,028-foot summit. Wood was almost twenty percent lighter than normal because of calories burned during the climb. They spent about twenty minutes at the top before having to head down because the sun was setting.

Their descent was not anti-climactic. In order to keep supplies to a minimum, Wood and Congdon only used oxygen tanks on the final twelve-hour section of the climb, and on their descent. However, Congdon's tanks ran out of oxygen at 28,000 feet, which slowed him down. Wood moved ahead and, with the aid of a miner's light, made it back to the sixth camp at 2:00 A.M. Congdon finally arrived at 3:30 A.M., suffering frostbite from the severe cold. Then, while attempting to melt snow for drinking water, their stove exploded, burning Wood's face and making a hole in the tent. Wood threw the stove out the door and it dropped off a ledge and disappeared down the mountain. Though they went without food and water that night, Wood and Congdon made the rest of the descent the next day without any serious problems. A second climb was not attempted due to the exhaustion of the team.

RICK HANSEN—MAN IN MOTION

On March 21, 1985, Rick Hansen (born in 1957) set off on his "Man in Motion" World Tour from Vancouver's Oakridge shopping mall. Three hundred invited guests showed up for the festivities, but the crowd generally ignored his departure. However, like Terry Fox and Steve Fonyo, the two young men who inspired him, Rick Hansen has since inspired Canada and the world as he has wheeled his way across the world.

In the summer of 1973, Hansen was permanently paralyzed from the waist down when the pickup truck he was riding in went out of control and rolled over, breaking his back and severing his spine. He started thinking about wheeling around the world in 1974, when he was 16, but it would not be until December of 1983 that he would begin to put his plan into action. During those nine years, Hansen completed his high school and university education (in physical education), and became a four-time winner of the World Wheelchair Championships. He also won national titles in wheelchair volleyball and basketball and nineteen international marathons, including the Boston Marathon in 1983. He was a finalist in the fifteen-hundred-meter wheelchair competition at the 1984 Olympics at Los Angeles.

Beginning in the fall of 1984, Hansen and Timothy Frick,

who had coached him in wheelchair sports since 1977, started shaping the tour. While Hansen trained, they worked hard over the next four months at the difficult job of raising money. His goal was to wheel 25,845 miles (40,073 kilometers), equal to the circumference of the earth, and raise ten million dollars for spinal cord research, rehabilitation, and wheelchair sports. Finally setting off on March 21, 1985, Hansen and his seven-member crew would not return to Canada for seventeen months. He wheeled through thirty-four countries, across four continents, five mountain ranges, through a flood, wheeling fifty miles (eighty kilometers) three out of every four days. In the trip he used five wheelchairs, wore out eighty pairs of gloves and had a hundred flat tires. Arriving at Cape Spear, Newfoundland on August 25, 1986, the crew began the Canadian portion of the tour, tracing the steps of Terry Fox and Steve Fonyo. Hansen received a hero's welcome when he arrived in Ottawa on October 26, 1986, as thousands of people gathered on Parliament Hill to greet him and Prime Minister Brian Mulroney gave him a government check for $1 million.

The tour crossed the British Columbia border on March 20, 1987, almost two years to the day since Hansen had set off from Vancouver. On May 22, 1987, Hansen arrived back at Vancouver's Oakridge mall from where he had left twenty-six months before. Seven thousand spectators greeted him in a welcome-home ceremony that was broadcast live across the country, an overwhelming number compared with the three hundred invited guests who had seen him off in 1985. He had made it! And though all but twenty-eight thousand dollars of the fourteen million dollars the marathon raised was contributed by Canadians, the generosity of the countries along the way kept the tour's operating costs down to $1.5 million. The funds are to be allocated by a special committee as grants from about a million dollars' worth of yearly interest from the trust fund.

In 1987, Hansen won a Manning Award for his contribution to the world's increased awareness of the abilities of the disabled, and for his innovative perception of a way to cause major change in social attitudes, and his courage and determination to make it happen. The cash awards have been presented annually since 1982 by the Ernest C. Manning Awards Foundation to stimulate, encourage, and support innovations by Canadians.

Transportation

STEAMER CROSSES ATLANTIC

Canada has many achievements in steamer travel and use, attributable in part to the efforts of Samuel Cunard (1787-1865). Cunard and two hundred shareholders in the Quebec and Halifax Steam Navigation Company commissioned the building of a steamship that would establish several firsts in maritime history, the *Royal William*, in Quebec in 1831. It was designed by a young Scots-Canadian named John Gordie and built under his supervision at the Black and Campbell shipyard in Quebec City, with its twin side-lever engines built by Messrs Bennet and Henderson of Montreal. The boat was launched at Cape Cove, Quebec on April 27 of that year, and was intended to run a scheduled route between Quebec and Halifax. The experiment was unsuccessful and the ship was sold in 1833. It was used for towing and excursions and on one trip became the first steamship to visit an American port — Boston — flying the Union Jack. The new owners decided to sell the vessel and not finding buyers in North America they decided to sail it across the Atlantic. On August 5, 1833, the *Royal William* left Quebec for Pictou, Nova Scotia, to be loaded with coal. Leaving Pictou on August 18 with seven passengers, the steamship arrived in Gravesend, England twenty-five days later, on September 11, the first vessel to cross the Atlantic Ocean wholly under steam power (with brief intervals for boiler scraping). Although at least two steamships had made the trip earlier, both had made most of the voyage under sail with their steam engines shut down. The *Royal William* was sold to the Spanish navy in 1834 and renamed the *Isabella Segunda*. It may have been the first steampowered naval warship in history, and on May 5, 1836 became the first steampowered warship to fire its guns in battle when it bombarded Carlist rebels at San Sebastian.

In 1839, Cunard founded the British and North American Royal Mail Steam Packet Company. He was able to obtain the British government contract to carry mail by steamship from England to Boston with a stop in Halifax. With this contract in hand, Cunard established a transatlantic steam service. On July, 17, 1840, Cunard's first scheduled steamer, the *Britannia*, arrived in Halifax with Cunard and his daughter aboard and then docked in Boston two days later.

Just over sixty years after Cunard launched the *Royal William*, on April 29, 1891, the Canadian Pacific Railway (C.P.R.)-owned steamship, the *Empress of India*, arrived in Vancouver from Yokohama as part of the by then regular transpacific steamship service. The steamer had made the crossing in record time, two days faster than the previous record. The C.P.R. had inaugurated the service with a leased steamship, the *Abyssinia*, that had originally been used by Cunard for North Atlantic service and then sold to another company. The *Abyssinia* made the inaugural run from Yokohama to Vancouver between May 31, 1887 and the evening of June 13, a voyage of thirteen days and fourteen hours. In 1903 and 1904, the world's first steam turbine ocean liners, the *Victorian* and the *Virginian*, were built for the Allan Steamship Company of Montreal. These ships were the forerunners of today's turbine-driven passenger ocean liners.

AUTOMATIC LUBRICATORS—THE REAL McCOY

On May 2, 1844, Elijah McCoy was born in Colchester, Upper Canada (now the province of Ontario, Canada). The son of fugitive slaves George and Mildred McCoy, who escaped from Kentucky through the Underground Railroad, Elijah would go on to revolutionize the operation of machinery with his inventions. After raising Elijah on a farm in Colchester, the McCoy family left Canada and moved back to the United States after the Civil War, settling in a place about one mile from Ypsilanti, Michigan. George McCoy opened a cigar manufacturing firm and used the profits to send Elijah to Edinburgh, Scotland to complete an apprenticeship in mechanical engineering. Since he was a young boy Elijah had shown an interest in machines and things mechanical.

In 1870, Elijah returned to Ypsilanti as a full-fledged mechanical engineer, but met with racial prejudice and was forced to take a job as a fireman for the Michigan Central Railroad. He operated a small machine shop on the side, but his main job involved shovelling coal for the trains' steam engines, and oiling all the moving parts of the trains. At that time, trains and all other machinery had to be shut down periodically so that the moving parts could be oiled or lubricated.

McCoy became interested in the problems of lubricating machinery, as he saw the frequent shutting down of engines and other machines for oiling and lubricating as a waste of both time and money. In his machine shop he began working on various devices that would lubricate machines as they worked. The idea was to build into the machine canals to carry lubricant to the parts of the machine that needed it. On July 12, 1872, McCoy received the patent for his first invention, an automatic lubricator for steam engines, patent #129,843. The lubricator consisted of a cup that held oil that was built in as part of the steam cylinder; the bottom of the cup was attached to a hollow rod and the opening closed off by a valve; the cup released oil into the cylinder automatically when the engine's steam pressure pushed a piston up through the rod opening the valve. A year later, McCoy improved upon his original design so that the lubricator oiled the cylinder at the most important time, when the steam was exhausted.

In 1873, he married Mary Delaney, and they moved to Detroit in 1882. He opened up Elijah McCoy Manufacturing Co. in Detroit with white friends and promoters and acted as Vice-President for the company. Further improvements patented by McCoy in later years numbered fifty-seven in all for lubricating systems for heavy machinery used in locomotives, steamboats and ocean liners. He also invented an ironing board, a lawn sprinkler, a wagon tongue support, and a rubber heel for shoes—eighty-seven inventions in total. By 1892, his lubricating cups were used in factories everywhere, on all railroads in the West and on steamers on the Great Lakes. Eventually, no piece of heavy machinery was considered complete unless it had the "McCoy system." Buyers of machinery would always inspect to make sure McCoy's lubricators were part of the deal. From this concern for quality in automatic lubricators comes the now widely known saying, "the real McCoy."

Unfortunately for Elijah McCoy, this fame did not prevent him from losing control of his investments and inventions. While others made millions from his lubricating systems, McCoy lost his business and his home after his wife's death in 1923 and was committed to Wayne County (Eloise) Hospital in 1928, where he died penniless on October 10, 1929.

TRANSCONTINENTAL RAILWAY

Canada operates two transcontinental railway companies, Canadian Pacific Railway (C.P.R.) and Canadian National Railways. The process that brought these companies into being began with Sir John A. Macdonald's promise to British Columbia that the railway would be built as a condition of British Columbia joining the country. On May 7, 1872, the government introduced the Canadian Pacific Railroad Bill, calling for the line to be completed from the Pacific to a point near Lake Nipissing, Manitoba within ten years. The C.P.R. General Charter, which authorized the construction of the railway, was passed on June 14 of that year. However, the government under Macdonald resigned on November 5, 1873 when evidence was presented that members had accepted campaign monies from Hugh Allan in return for the railway construction contract.

The new government under Alexander Mackenzie continued the process by appointing the Royal Commission on the Canadian Pacific Railway on August 18, 1873. The first session of the third Parliament met on March 26, 1874 and passed an Act providing for the construction of the C.P.R. but a worldwide depression prevented construction from beginning in British Columbia until May 14, 1880, under the direction of Andrew Onderdenk. Macdonald had been back in office since 1878 and had awarded the contract to a new private group that included officials of the Hudson's Bay Company and the Bank of Montreal. The private company was incorporated as the Canadian Pacific Railway on February 15, 1881. The difficulties of construction were helped by government subsidies that included twenty-five million dollars in cash, twenty-five million acres in a belt along the railway, and thirty-seven million dollars worth of surveys. Construction continued until the last spike was driven by Donald Smith at Craigellachie, in Eagle Pass, British Columbia on November 7, 1885. When completed, the railway stretched 2,891 miles (4,652 kilometers) from Montreal to Port Moody, B.C, 993 miles (1600 kilometers) longer than the first U.S. transcontinental railway.

The Canadian National Railways was created in 1919 as a Crown (government) Corporation. Over the next four years the company took over five financially troubled railway systems. On October 4, 1922 the separate lines were consolidated into one system with a new board of directors, with Sir Henry Thornton as president, forming the new transcontinental Canadian National Railways. The company (now called CN Rail) is Canada's largest railroad and the longest railway system in North America, controlling 31,050 miles (50,000 kilometers) of track in Canada and the United States. The company is one of the world's major transportation and communication systems.

The railway has also provided passenger rail service since its completion in 1885. Since 1977, passenger rail service has been provided through the Crown (government-owned) corporation Via Rail. However, in a decision that Prime Minister Brian Mulroney argued was made "to save Via Rail," the federal Transport Minister Benoît Bouchard announced drastic cutbacks in Via Rail's operations on October 4, 1989. The reductions, which took effect beginning on January 15, 1990, eliminated eighteen of Via's thirty-eight routes entirely, cut back on many other routes, decreased its operations from four hundred and five passenger trains weekly to one hundred ninety-one, and laid off about two thousand eight hundred Via workers.

Many critics of the government's decision believe the intent behind the decision is to eliminate Via completely. The direct cause of the reductions was Ottawa's decision to decrease Via's 1989 subsidy of five hundred and sixty-one million dollars to three hundred and fifty million dollars by 1992. Of three legal challenges to the decision by two provincial governments, more than twenty municipalities and several other organizations and individuals, only one succeeded as a British Columbia court on January 19,1990 ordered Via to maintain one Vancouver Island route for at least another year, based on the provincial government's argument that the route was guaranteed by the "spirit" of British Columbia's entry into Confederation. Across the country in 1989, polls showed that seventy-four percent of Canadians believed that the government's decision was the first step in getting rid of passenger rail service altogether, an institution that had linked one coast with the other for one hundred and four years.

F IRST ROTARY SNOWPLOUGH AND SNOWBLOWER

Up to 1885, railroads used a wedge-plough attached to the front of the train to remove snowdrifts, avalanche debris and other obstructions. In 1869, Toronto dentist J.W. Elliot took out a patent on the "Compound Revolving Snow Shovel." However, Elliot, like many other Canadian inventors, was unable to interest any Canadian investors in the plough. The first working model of the plough was eventually built in 1883-84 by Leslie Brothers of Orangeville under the supervision of an inventor named Orange Jull. It was tested in the Canadian Pacific Railway Parkdale yards in Toronto. The Elliot-Jull snowplough soon became standard equipment on trains in North America and in many parts of the world. The plough now in use is derived from the original design, which was standardized in 1911.

In 1925-26, Arthur Sicard demonstrated his new invention, the snowblower, for the first time. Sicard grew up on a Canadian farm at St. Leonard de Port Maurice, Quebec and after coping with the hazardous conditions of the Canadian winter all his life, he conceived the idea of the snow removal machine to keep roads and highways clear. He worked with a thresher on the farm as a boy and incorporated the rotating blades of the thresher into his design for the snowblower. He was not able to get any financial support for his invention initially but through sheer determination and hard work he was able to save enough money to concentrate on promoting and perfecting his product. Finally, after its successful demonstration in the winter of 1925-26, the idea caught on; snowblowers he built were purchased by cities in Quebec, by the Department of Transport in Ottawa and eventually came into use throughout the world.

LONGEST COVERED BRIDGE IN THE WORLD

Located at Hartland, New Brunswick, northwest of Fredericton, is the longest covered bridge in the world. Construction on the bridge began in 1897 and was completed two years later. The bridge is 1,282 feet in length (390.8 meters), longer than the channel spanned by either the Queensboro (1909) or Tappan Zee (1956) bridges (both uncovered) in New York.

THE HYDROFOIL BOAT

Another invention that Alexander Graham Bell (1847-1922) was involved in is the hydrofoil boat. Working in the summer of 1908 with Casey Baldwin at the Bell laboratory on Baddeck Bay, Nova Scotia, Bell developed one of the first successful hydrofoil boats. The idea of a hydrofoil boat had been tested as far back as 1861 in England, and later in France, Italy, and the United States. That summer and fall, changing the boat's design almost every day, and testing it over and over, Bell and Baldwin came up with a configuration that is essentially the same as that used in some hydrofoil boats today.

The key to their design was what Baldwin called "Reefing Hydrocurves", the submerged sets of wings which supported the boat and lifted the large upper surfaces of the boat's hull out of the water first, once a certain speed was reached, thereby decreasing the water resistance and making high speeds relatively easy to reach. Bell and Baldwin could not overcome the size and weight of motors at that time, however, which made it impossible for their hydrofoils to keep the boat off the water for extended lengths of time. They continued their research in 1911 when improved aircraft engines were available, but the beginning of World War I interrupted the experiments. However, when the United States entered the war in 1917, the experiments began again, as Bell was convinced that hydrofoil boats could be used to pursue submarines. Further improvements in aircraft engines allowed them to use, by 1919, airplane propellers driven by two four-hundred-horsepower Liberty engines, supplied by the United States Navy. That summer their boat, called the H.D.4, reached the world-record speed of 70.86 miles per hour (113.37

kilometers), a record which wasn't broken until 1929.

F IRSTS IN AIRCRAFT
STOL (Short take-off and landing aircraft)

Since the 1940s, Canada has been a pioneer in the manufacturing of low-speed, low-flying aircraft (at altitudes of twenty thousand to thirty thousand feet (6,096 meters to 9,144 meters)) capable of landing on short runways (less than two thousand feet long (609.6 meters)). STOL aircraft are also much quieter than standard designs. The Beaver, the first true STOL aircraft, was delivered for use by de Havilland Canada in 1948. The Turbo-Beaver, Otter and Twin Otter, Caribou and Buffalo were also designed with STOL characteristics by de Havilland Canada. Developed for use by bush pilots and the military, it was realized in the 1960's that STOL aircraft could also reduce the time and energy spent getting to and from airports by making downtown airports feasible. In a demonstration of the assets of STOL aircraft in 1966 that came to be known as Metro 66, four hundred and forty takeoffs and landings were held at eight different downtown Manhattan sites without any damage to aircraft, personnel or property. The largest contingent of the more than forty aircraft involved was provided by de Havilland Canada. Studies began in both the U.S. and Canada in 1967 to link cities along STOL routes.

In 1971, the Canadian Department of Transport authorized the development of a STOL commuter service for demonstration. By 1973, the U.S. Civil Aeronautics Board was forced to terminate its plans for a Northeast Corridor STOL project, and Canada decided to proceed on its own. A STOL service called Airtransit, operated as a subsidiary of Air Canada and flying between Ottawa and Montreal, began service on July 24, 1974 using six specially modified de Havilland Twin Otters. It was an immediate success and cut downtown-to-downtown air travel time from two hours to one hour and twenty-five minutes.

Today the Dash-7, a commuter or regional airliner, is in use in over 107 countries around the world, the largest user being the United States. Since 1974, half-hourly flights between Ottawa and Montreal have been featured by Airtransit, and the planes used are 12-passenger de Havilland Canada Twin Otters.

First aircraft built for the north

In 1935-36 at Montreal, Robert Noorduyn began designing and
manufacturing the Norseman , a high-wing, single engine plane and
the first successful Canadian-designed aircraft built for use in the
north. Although other aircraft had proved useful in opening up
Canada's northern regions, they were designed for more hospitable
climates and were modified for use in the north. Aviators across the
world have favored the Norseman for its performance over rugged
country and short take-off and landing capability. It was the first
Canadian designed aircraft to find a significant market outside of
Canada.

First commercial jet transport

The first commercial jet transport to fly in the Western Hemisphere,
the "Jetliner" C-102, was designed in Canada by James Floyd, an
Englishman. Built by Avro of Toronto, it was first flown on August
10,1949 over the Malton airport outside Toronto, the first flight of a
jet transport in North America, and the second in the world by only
two weeks. In a record-breaking seventy-five minute flight from
Toronto to New York on April 18, 1950, the Jetliner carried the first
airmail ever carried by a jet-powered aircraft and made the first
international jet-transport flight in North America. The flight generated great interest in the United States and was one of the outstanding aeronautical achievements of its day. A U.S. syndicated column
reported on the event as follows: "This should give our nation a good
healthful kick in its placidity. The fact that our massive but under-
populated good neighbor to the north has a mechanical product that
licks anything of ours is just what the doctor ordered for our over-
developed ego. The Canadian plane's feat accelerates a process
already begun in this nation—a realization that Uncle Sam has no
monopoly on genius, that our products are not necessarily the best
simply because we made them." In recognition, Floyd was awarded
the Wright Medal for the Jetliner, the first person who was not a U.S.
citizen ever to win it.

However, the plane was never produced commercially for
a variety of reasons, none of them convincing enough to warrant the
abandoning of a ten million dollar project that had produced the first
and foremost jetliner in North America. The outbreak of the Korean

War in the 1950s persuaded Minister of Defence Production C.D. Howe that Avro should concentrate on producing the CF-100 fighter plane. The Jetliner was sold for scrap in 1956, and only the nose section and engines still exist in the National Aviation Museum in Ottawa.

The Avro Arrow

With the historical perspective afforded by the fiasco of scrapping the Avro Jetliner, the saga of the Avro Arrow seems to be a comic-tragedy. In 1952, the Royal Canadian Air Force decided to continue the program that had successfully produced the CF 100, Canada's first "home-designed and built front-line fighter" plane. Two years later, the preliminary design of the CF 105, known as the Arrow, was submitted by Avro. Skipping over the prototype stage of design, Avro produced a pre-production-type aircraft in just four years. The first flight took place on March 25, 1958, and the Arrow was almost immediately hailed as perhaps the most advanced jet interceptor in existence. It seemed that the Arrow would make a lasting mark on world technology for Canada.

However, on February 20, 1959, Prime Minister Diefenbaker announced that the Avro Arrow program was cancelled, citing cost and the government's feeling that the fighter was obsolete. The six Arrow aircraft that had been built were destroyed. The Avro plant in Malton was closed down, and the company's research team dispersed to other companies and occupations.

VARIABLE PITCH PROPELLER

Without the variable pitch propeller the air transport industry, quite literally, could not have gotten off the ground. Called "one of the most important developments in the whole history of aviation," the variable pitch propeller allowed the pilot to alter the length and slant of the propeller blades while in motion, increasing efficiency. Before 1920, aircraft could fly but could not carry heavy payloads that would require extra fuel for the flight. The propellers of the time were well-suited for take-off needs but they could not be adjusted when the plane was in flight. Wallace Rupert Turnbull (1870-1954) solved this problem. An aeronautical engineer born in Saint John, New Brunswick, Turnbull built the first working model of the propeller in England in 1916 and brought it to Canada in 1918. He exhibited the propeller at the New York Inventions Show in February 1923 and won a silver medal. Ground tests at Camp Borden, Ontario followed and in 1925 Turnbull completed a second design of the propeller. The second design was given flight tests at Camp Borden on June 29, 1927.

Because Turnbull's innovation allowed greater loads to be carried with efficiency and safety, aircraft companies were able to earn money for the first time and survive without direct government subsidies. The money earned could go into the development of new airplanes and allowed the formation of the basis of the air transport industry that thrives today. Although Turnbull has been called the "father of aeronautical research in Canada," he lacked the flair for self-advertisement and publicity, and remains one of the world's most important unknown aeronautical engineers. However, after Alexander Graham Bell, Turnbull is probably Canada's most success-ful private inventor. He managed to earn a living, if not an interna-tional reputation, solely by inventing. In 1929, Turnbull sold the rights to the variable pitch propeller to the Curtiss-Wright Manufac-turing Company in the United States and the British rights to the Bristol Aeroplane Company of England.

FIRST COMMERCIALLY SUCCESSFUL SNOWMOBILE

In 1922, mechanic Joseph-Armand Bombardier invented the first "snowmobile" (*autoneige* in French), a propeller driven sled. The initial design was for a one- or two-person snowmobile, which he called the "Husky," but it would be some time yet before the ma-chines began to replace sled dogs. The Mounties resisted the change until 1969, when the expense of keeping dogs was cited as a factor in the switch.

Several years passed before Bombardier's ideas would be incorporated into the modern machine. The first commercially successful snowmobile was the B-7 Bombardier Snowmobile, built by Bombardier and patented on June 29, 1937. Little more than a car placed upon skis and half-tracks, the machine seated seven and cost around seventy-five hundred dollars. He sold fifty models and they were used as buses and for medical transport in the winter.

The heavy weight of most engines prevented further development of Bombardier's idea until 1958, when he found a light two-stroke, single cylinder engine in Austria that weighed less than thirty pounds. The following winter, on November 9, 1959, the first 250 snowmobiles, which Bombardier intended to call "Ski-dogs" but changed the name to "Ski-doos", rolled off the assembly line at Bombardier's plant at Valcourt, Quebec (near Sherbrooke). In 1971, 226,000 Ski-doos were sold in North America.

The fascination with travelling over snow must have run in the Bombardier family: the first Canadian to reach the North Pole by snowmobile was Jean-Luc Bombardier, a nephew of Joseph Bombardier.

A NTI-GRAVITY SUIT

Called the father of aviation medicine, Dr. Wilbur R. Franks (1901-86) was a wing commander in World War II and became Director of Aviation Medical Research for the Royal Canadian Air Force (RCAF). Familiar with the forces of gravity that caused pilots to black out while pulling out of dives and doing other maneuvers, Dr. Franks developed a suit with a tongue-twister of a name: Franks Flying Suit. In 1940, Franks and his colleagues at the University of Toronto invented the anti-gravity outfit, the world's first pressurized suit. The suit was constructed by a team at the Banting and Best Medical Research Institute at the university. The original prototype of the space suits worn by astronauts, the suit was made of rubber with pads full of water laced onto the legs. The fluid and the pressurized rubber garment counteracted the forces of gravity and the suit was used extensively and successfully by pilots during World War II. The principles of its construction proved invaluable in the subsequent design of space suits.

T RANS-CANADA HIGHWAY— Longest national highway in the world

April 25, 1950 must have been a banner day for asphalt companies. On that day the first steps were taken toward construction of the longest paved road in the world. Governments of the provinces of Ontario, Manitoba, Saskatchewan, Alberta, British Columbia (B.C.), and Prince Edward Island signed an agreement with the federal government ensuring the construction of the Trans-Canada Highway. Negotiations had been ongoing since the Trans-Canada Highway Act was given Royal Assent on December 10, 1949.

Saskatchewan was the first province to complete its portion of the highway, and on August 23, 1957, the province's premier, T.C. Douglas, opened the four hundred and six mile (six hundred fifty-four kilometer) section of road. The federal government and the government of Quebec signed an agreement on October 27, 1960 for the construction of the Quebec section of the highway. On September 3, 1962, the highway was officially opened, although all the sections were not yet completed, in a ceremony at Rogers Pass, Glacier National Park, British Columbia. The Ontario section of the highway, stretching from Fort Frances east to Atikokan, was not opened until June 28, 1965.

The road now crosses the country, stretching four thousand eight hundred sixty miles (seven thousand eight hundred twenty-one kilometers) from St. John's, Newfoundland to Victoria, British Columbia.

Longest street in the world

The longest designated street in the world is Yonge Street which runs north and west from Toronto, Ontario. When the first segment of the street was completed in 1796, it was about thirty-four miles long (about fifty-five kilometers). Now the street officially runs all the way to Rainy River at the Ontario-Minnesota border and is 1,178.3 miles (1,900.5 kilometers) long.

F OREMOST ANTI-POLLUTION CARS

Facts do not cease to exist because they are ignored, but sometimes it may seem like it. In August 1972, a joint United States-Canadian competition was held to determine the best design of an urban vehicle, with pollution considerations and energy use paramount. There were sixty-three working entries in the event, sponsored by the Transportation Development Agency (now Centre) of the Canadian Ministry of Transport and four U.S. institutes of technology. Two of the concerns that prompted the design of these research vehicles were the ineffective car models, many of them designed in the United States, that dominated the market, and a report in which the New York State Department of Environmental Conservation had identified cars as the factor responsible for forty percent by weight of all urban pollution. Concerns about energy use formed another reason for initiating the competition.

The purpose of the design competition was two-fold: to create a better vehicle that would encourage both U.S. and Canadian companies to take up the innovations, and especially to prompt Canadian companies to enter the automobile manufacturing industry with domestic models. Requirements of the competition specified that the cars were to be ten feet long and able to carry two passengers, travel 50 miles (80.50 kilometers) on a single tank of gas, complete a course of 4.4 miles (7.09 kilometers) and be as inexpensive, quiet and non-polluting as possible.

The two award-winning cars were both Canadian entries. The entry by the University of British Columbia received the top award for overall excellence according to the various criteria. It won in the safety and style categories and scored well in the other tests including emission of pollutants, estimated cost of production, space utilization, driveability, fuel efficiency, and bumper effectiveness. The entry by the University of Western Ontario and Fanshaw College of Applied Arts and Technology in London, Ontario, won the award for the best electric vehicle as well as the most points for student innovation.

The entry by the University of British Columbia solved the emissions problem by using a platinum catalytic converter that acts upon carbon monoxide and converts it to relatively harmless carbon dioxide. The car also included a convenience device that featured automatic readouts for tire pressure, brake wear, and wheel alignment. Two decades later many of these innovations remain on the drawing boards in Canada and the United States, while significant car improvements continue to come from imported vehicles from other countries. And Canadians have yet to develop their award-winning ideas into a domestic production line-vehicle.

Energy

FIRSTS IN THE OIL INDUSTRY
Development of kerosene

Canada has had many firsts in the oil industry, many of which transformed life in North America. Dr. Abraham Gesner (1797-1864) of Halifax recorded an early achievement in this field with his development of what he called "kerosene", a term he coined from two Greek words meaning "wax" and "oil." Originally trained in medicine, Gesner's true love was geology. When he was dismissed from his job as a Provincial Geologist in 1842, "in the interest of economy", he tried various employments, including setting up Canada's first museum, but nothing seemed to work out for him. His geological interests persisted, however, extending from the geological survey he had completed of New Brunswick from 1838 to 1843.

In 1846, Gesner's kerosene was first demonstrated in Charlottetown, Prince Edward Island. In 1854, he patented the process he had developed for distilling kerosene from a coal-like mineral now known as albertite (named after Albert Co. New Brunswick, where the largest deposit was found). Though it had a terrible odor, the first "coal-oil", as Canadians came to call kerosene, burned brightly, eclipsing the smokey flames of whale-oil lamps, burning fat, seal oil or tallow candles, all of which were difficult to read by. Before kerosene, night lighting was limited to these alternatives, unless you took a chance with your life and used "burning fluid", a mixture of alcohol and turpentine, that lit and burned many houses to the ground. The new source of light was first used in a lighthouse.

As well as being called the father of night-life, Gesner may well be called the forefather of today's multi-billion dollar petrochemical industry. However, he did not benefit financially from his achievements because a Scottish chemist, James Young, had developed a similar fuel in England and obtained a British patent for what he called "parafinne-oil" in 1850. Although Gesner's work preceded Young's, his patent did not and thereafter Gesner had to pay royalties to Young for the right to use his own process.

First oil company in North America

The year Abraham Gesner patented his distillation process for kerosene, asphalt was first marketed in North America by Charles and Henry Tripp, of Oil Springs, a village in Enniskillen Township, south of Sarnia, Ontario. The first oil company in North America, the International Petroleum and Mining Company of Hamilton C.W., was founded by Charles Tripp in 1854, about four weeks before the Pennsylvania Rock Oil Co. was founded in the United States.

First commercial oil well in North America

In 1856, James Miller Williams, a Hamilton carriage maker, took over the the oil company described above that was started by the Tripp brothers. He proceeded to dig the first commercial oil well in North America in Enniskillen Township, Ontario, and it went into production on 1858, one year before Edwin L. Drake successfully drilled for oil in Pennsylvania. This accomplishment earned him the title of father of the American oil industry, for he had discovered a large enough oil deposit to justify the construction of the first oil refinery in Canada at Hamilton in 1860. Williams was awarded two bronze plaques in England for being the first man in America to produce an oil well and the first man in the world to transform crude oil into lamp oil. A replica of one of the company wells now stands near the Oil Museum of Canada, which opened at Oil Springs in 1959.

FIRST PUBLICLY OWNED ELECTRIC UTILITY (ONTARIO HYDRO)
First plant to run on hydro-electricity in the world

Electricity was first used for lighting in Canada in 1877 by the Montreal Harbour Commission to light the city's waterfront. In 1888, John R. Barber's paper mill in Georgetown, Ontario was the first plant in the world to run on hydro-electric power. But the full development of hydro-electricity for the public's use began in the early 1900's, when the leading businessmen and politicians in a number of smaller cities in Ontario began to fear that if hydroelectric power development in the province fell into the hands of a few giant companies, their cities might be denied access to an abundant supply of cheap power needed to support the development of an industrial base. They demanded an investigation by the provincial government, which is responsible in Canada for controlling and developing natural resources. The then Liberal government responded by setting up the Snider Commission to study the idea of municipal power cooperatives, and gave the interested municipalities the power to select the commissioners and hire technical experts. In 1905, a provincial election saw the Conservatives topple the thirty-four year old Liberal government. The new Premier, J.P. Whitney, who had advocated public power while in opposition, moved quickly to establish the Hydro-Electric Power Commission of Inquiry on July 5, 1905.

The three men who comprised the commission, Adam Beck, P.W. Ellis (both of whom served on the Snider Commission), and George Pattinson began a comprehensive survey of developed and undeveloped hydroelectric resources in the province. They requested the power companies' cooperation in giving information to the commission about their costs and rates, but the companies at first refused and then gave an inconsistent picture of their business practices.

Over the next eight months both commissions compiled their reports. The Snider Commission's report, released on March 28, 1906, recommended that a municipal cooperative build and operate transmission lines linking Niagara to the major towns in Ontario. The first section of the Beck Commission's report was released on April 4, 1906. On May 14, 1906, following the recommendations of the Beck Commission's report, the Hydro-Electric Commission of Ontario was incorporated by an Act of the Provincial Legislature to generate, supply and deliver its own electric power throughout Ontario. On June 7, 1906, Adam Beck (1857-1925) was appointed the first chairman of the corporation, known as Ontario Hydro since 1974. As a proponent of "power for the people", he had led the battle for the public ownership of the source of electrical power and continued to do so during his nineteen years as chairman, until his death on August 15, 1925. The Commission was first set up to regulate the private companies but Beck managed to drive most of the private competitors out of business, using the Commission's power of expropriation and control over private company rates, and expand the Commission to fill the gap. In so doing, the Commission became the first nationalized (publicly-owned) electrical utility in the world. In 1908, two years after the Commission was created, it signed an agreement with twelve municipalities to supply them with electricity at cost. A testimony to Beck's tenacity as chairman is that by 1923 the Commission was the largest utility in the world and by 1925 it had supply agreements with some 247 municipalities.

Unfortunately, the results of Beck's decisions usually involved huge expenditures of money, so that by 1923 Hydro already accounted for half the province's debt. The Legislature's annual audits of Hydro since 1915 had failed to give them any control over the utility. The expansion continued after Beck's death, as the new Hydro chairman, Charles A. McGrath, convinced the provincial premier that an impending power shortage would hurt the province's economy and that contracts had to be signed with power companies in Quebec in order to ensure an adequate supply. The Depression and a provincial election led to the Liberals taking over the provincial Legislature again in 1934, and to the cancellation of the Quebec power contracts in 1935, but soon afterwards another "impending" power shortage led to the restoration of the contracts.

The expansion continued from 1940 to 1980, and throughout Hydro's public image remained relatively untarnished. The reason was simple: though it did not act like a truly "public" utility in many ways, it had met its basic goal of bringing cheap, reliable electric power to the service of every Ontarian. However, Hydro's prediction about future electricity needs decreased significantly by the early 1980s under pressure from the Legislature, a government commission studying Hydro's plans, and public interest groups. At the same time, Hydro's debt, rates, and cost overruns all increased. By 1989, Ontario Hydro had agreements to supply electricity to three hundred and sixteen municipalities serving 2.4 million customers, one hundred and five large industrial customers and fifty rural distribution systems to service eight hundred thousand rural retail customers located in areas not served by the municipal utilities. After the Tennessee Valley Authority, Hydro is the second largest utility company in North America. It now derives about forty-three percent of its power from nuclear stations, thirty-seven percent from fossil fuels (primarily coal), and twenty percent from hydro-electricity. Whether the utility will meet its mandate to provide power to its customers at the lowest feasible cost (financial, social and environmental) remains an issue as we move into the 1990s.

FIRSTS IN LIGHTING
First light bulb

Canada has two achievements in the development of light bulbs, both inextricably linked to developments in the same field in the United States. The first achievement involves Henry Woodward, a medical student from Toronto, Ontario who is remarkably unknown to the general public. In 1874, Woodward patented the first incandescent lamp with an electric light bulb, testing it successfully at 87 Woodward Street in Toronto. However, Henry sold a share in the patent in 1875 to Thomas Edison, and in 1879 Edison managed to come up with a more practical lamp that efficiently transmitted electricity into a lightbulb.

Development of the "Light Pipe"

The second achievement involves a reversal of the what happened to Woodward. In 1882, an American named William Wheeler designed and patented a system for piping light, using copper tubing and mirrors. However, the patent issue did not include a working model of his invention, and in fact it didn't work. Nearly a hundred years later, in 1979, Lorne Whitehead, a graduate student in physics at the University of British Columbia, invented the "Light Pipe", a very precise, efficient and practical prismatic device that put Wheeler's idea to work. In Whitehead's case, history is being made right now.

Frustrated with the poor quality of fluorescent lighting in the basement of the physics lab at the university, Whitehead designed the Light Pipe, not realizing that Wheeler had preceded him with the idea. However, the Light Pipe uses a hollow, rectangular acrylic tube that is covered with minute, finely angulated prisms; when a light source is put at one end of the tube, the light is reflected and transmitted down the tube's entire length. Whitehead realized that if he could make the prisms accurate enough, the light would be practical and could be manufactured.

That turned out to be possible, and after patenting his invention in 1980, Whitehead opened up TIR (Total Internal Reflection) Systems in Vancouver in April, 1983. The Light Pipe has been hailed as an alternative to fluorescent lighting, which for years has caused complaints about headaches and tired eyes. It delivers a gentle, even light that does not use fluorescence. TIR Systems Ltd. has grown into a million dollar business that employs thirty people and is expanding rapidly. The light's range in size from small custom lighting designs to factories and open-plan malls. There is a very high level of interest in their product in Europe where some sales have already been made. The company is recognized worldwide as the leader in lighting technology developments and, remarkably, it has remained Canadian-owned and operated. It is also a good example of a business created by a technology transfer from a University of British Columbia development. In 1984, Whitehead won a Manning Principle Award for his invention and development of the lighting system.

The Light Pipe has dozens of practical applications. Special lighting effects are easy to achieve with color filters, and these effects were evident at the fifty-foot-high Light Pipe arches that marked the monorail at Expo 86 in Vancouver. Light Pipes also highlight the Park Avenue Tower in New York City, One Minnesota Center near Minneapolis, the Bakery Center retail and theater complex in South Miami; and Europe's tallest commercial building , the eighty-story Messeturm Frankfurt project in Frankfurt, Germany. They are also used for lighting hazardous areas, where the heat of a normal light bulb or potential sparks from light sources could cause a problem, cold storage area lighting, where servicing a light can be difficult, and security lighting. In each case, the light is "piped in" from a light source located in another part of the building. Light Pipes are also used for building highlighting, such as the forty-foot

Light Pipe pyramid atop the new IBM building in New York City.

Finally, after preliminary experiments, the Light Pipe is being used successfully at a North York, Ontario office building to beam natural sunlight into the top floors of the building as the light source for those offices. The prisms in the pipes are controlled by computers to keep the transmission of the sunlight constant. Considering that each watt of sunlight provides more illumination than five watts of electricity, the possibilities for energy-efficient lighting using the Light Pipe seem to be well worth developing.

Communication

FIRSTS IN NEWSPAPER PUBLISHING

The oldest paper in Canada is the *Halifax Gazette*. It was first issued on March 23, 1752 by John Bushell (1715-61), the first King's Printer in Halifax. Like all early papers, the *Gazette* existed only with government patronage and contained mainly government advertisements and official documents.

Bushell, who had come to Halifax from Boston, died in 1761 and his partner, German-born Anthony Henry, assumed his position as King's Printer and editor of the paper. However, the government dismissed Henry five years later for criticizing the Stamp Act, the law by which Britain taxed her colonies to pay for one-sixth of the cost of keeping troops garrisoned there.

As a result, the *Halifax Gazette* was replaced by the semi-official, subsidized *Nova Scotia Gazette*. This provided Henry with the opportunity for another first: he began printing a rival paper, the *Nova Scotia Chronicle and Weekly Advertiser*, the first paper printed independent of government patronage. The *Chronicle* took over the *Gazette* within a year and became in 1770 the *Nova Scotia Gazette and Weekly Chronicle*, once again with government patronage. Henry, as editor of the paper, resumed his role as King's Printer.

By 1778, Fleury Mesplet (1734-94) had begun publishing the first issues of *La Gazette de commerce et littéraire* in Montreal. It was the first entirely French newspaper in North America and survived initially, for just a year. In 1785, Mesplet started it up again and this time it enjoyed a long-successful run under the new name the *Montreal Gazette*, now one of the oldest newspapers still in existence in North America.

F REE MAIL

In Canada, you can send a letter to your member of Parliament while the government is in session without paying postage. Members of government may also send mail without postage to each other. Free mail, known as the Franking Privilege, was adopted in Canada in 1875 from the English system to facilitate communication between citizens and government. Franking Privilege also applies to books and other materials for the use of the blind, certain statistical surveys returned to Statistics Canada (the bureau of the Canadian government responsible for the collection of vital statistics) and certain documents concerning government business addressed to the Bank of Canada's head office or branch in Ottawa. Part of the actual statute reads as follows:

17. (1) Mailable matter addressed to or sent by the Governor General or sent by any department of the government of Canada is free of postage under such regulations as are made in that respect by the governor in Council.

(2) Mail shall be transmitted free of postage when sent to or by

(a) the speaker or clerk of the Senate or House of Commons at Ottawa, or

(b) a member of the Senate or House of Commons at Ottawa during a session of Parliament or during the ten days immediately preceding or following a session of Parliament.

U NDERWATER COMMUNICATIONS CABLES
First transatlantic cable

"The course of anything true never does run smooth," says a popular paraphrasing of Shakespeare. The same could be said of underwater cables. The word *telegraph* comes from the Greek for "to write far." In extending that distance across oceans, persistence seemed to be the key ingredient.

In 1852, engineer Frederic Newton Gisborne (1824-92) of St. John's, Newfoundland, using an insulated wire that was impervious to salt-water corrosion, began experimenting in underwater communications cables. He first tested the wire in 1852 by laying an undersea telegraph cable successfully from Cape Tormentine, New Brunswick to Carleton Head, Prince Edward Island, the first submarine cable in North America. Gisborne then conceived of the idea of establishing telegraphic communications between Europe and North America by way of Newfoundland.

He set about promoting his idea and was able to enlist the financial support of American investor Cyrus W. Field and the cooperation of the government of Newfoundland. This ensured the laying of another test cable in 1856 between Cape-Breton Island and Newfoundland. Although Gisborne was not involved, except in promoting the idea, the final step was one taken in ten-league boots by comparison—a transatlantic submarine cable for telegraphic purposes.

Trinity Bay, Newfoundland was chosen as the North American connection site for the cable, which made sense as it is the most easterly point in North America. Similarly, Ireland was chosen as the European connection site. Between August 7 and August 11, 1857, the first attempt was made to lay the cable. It failed. During the summer the following year, from July 7 to August 5, 1858, another attempt was made to lay the cable from Valentia, Ireland to Trinity Bay, Newfoundland. This time the cable worked. The first telegraphic message was sent from North America to Britain on August 16, 1858. It read: "Europe and America are united by telegraphy. Glory to God in the Highest, on earth peace, goodwill toward men." Unfortunately, a failure in the wire's insulation made the cable inoperative in October of that year. Another cable was successfully landed at Heart's Content, Newfoundland, on July 27, 1866.

Remarkably, North America was now connected with Europe, but Canada itself was not even connected telegraphically from coast to coast. However, the Canadian Pacific Railway (C.P.R.) telegraph was eventually completed, connecting the Atlantic with the Pacific, on January 24, 1885. The C.P.R. telegraph was connected with the transatlantic cable on December 18, 1889.

Longest submarine telephone cable

Next came the transpacific cable. On March 16, 1899, the fourth session of Canada's eighth Parliament met and passed the Pacific Cable Act. The Act provided for the laying of a cable from Canada to Australia and New Zealand. Canada's contribution to the Pacific cable construction was increased on March 6, 1901 to $2 million. In 1902, forty-four years after the first transatlantic cable had been laid, the transpacific cable was completed on October 31, connecting Vancouver, Canada and Brisbane, Australia.

On February 3, 1960, the government of Canada announced that Canada would contribute $25 million to the construction of a new Commonwealth transpacific cable. It would become the longest submarine telephone cable in the world, stretching from Sydney, Australia, via Norfolk Island, Fiji, and the Hawaiian Islands to Port Alberni, Canada . On December 19, 1961, the first link in the new round-the-world Commonwealth communications system, a transatlantic cable carrying voice, picture, and teletype messages, was inaugurated by Prime Minister Diefenbaker and Queen Elizabeth. The longest submarine telephone cable is called ANZCAN and is 9,415 miles long (15,629 kilometers).

ALEXANDER GRAHAM BELL AND THE TELEPHONE

Alexander Graham Bell (1847-1922), the inventor of the telephone, is one of recent history's great inventors, judging by the commercial and social significance of his invention, not to mention his numerous other inventions. Bell's family emigrated to Canada from Scotland in 1870, when he was twenty-three. They settled at Tutela Heights on the outskirts of Brantford, and although Bell moved to Boston soon afterward, in 1872, he often returned to Canada. The dispute concerning the "home" of the invention of the telephone was resolved by Bell in 1919 when he explained, "The telephone was conceived in Brantford in 1874 and born in Boston in 1875." Bell invented the telephone while trying to improve the telegraph system so that more than one message could be sent over a single wire. He perhaps had an advantage over the others who were working on this same development, for he was an expert in vocal physiology and acoustics, the third generation of his family to specialize in this field. In fact, the system that Professor Higgins uses in the musical *My Fair Lady* to transform the flower girl into a mysterious lady was invented by Bell's grandfather in Scotland.

The difference between Bell's telephone and the wire message systems was that the telephone had a continuous current, which varied in intensity in order to transmit sound. The telephone operated on the same principle as two rows of tuning forks placed parallel. When the note from one fork is struck, the corresponding fork will vibrate in sympathy with the sound generated by the first. In the same way, sound produced at one end of a telephone wire is replicated by the corresponding tuning fork at the other end.

First long-distance telephone call

The first telephone call from one building to another took place at Mt. Pleasant, Ontario on August 3, 1876 when Bell called his uncle David Bell at Brantford. One week later, on August 10, the first long-distance call was made between Brantford and Paris, Ontario, a distance of eight miles (thirteen kilometers). Both calls involved one-way communication, not two-way conversations.

Bell first offered his invention for marketing to a Canadian in 1875, selling the rights to George Brown, one of the Fathers of the Confederation, for three hundred dollars to be paid over six months. The money paid for the construction of the first telephone and Brown was enlisted by Bell to help him secure patent rights in England. However, Brown lost interest in the telephone and Bell, while waiting for Brown to secure his patent in England, almost lost his patent rights in the U.S. The American company, National Bell Telephone, organized in 1877, sent a man to Canada in 1880 to organize Bell Telephone of Canada. This is one of many cases in which a Canadian inventor had to go south of the border in order to get his invention developed and marketed, after being stymied by the skeptical and cautious minds of the Canadian business community.

In a speech to the telephone operators of America in 1911, Bell said, "I want to speak now of a very curious thing. In the case of new inventions we are generally led to believe that the public is ready to swallow anything, but that the grave scientific men are the most skeptical of all. I found just the opposite to be true in the case of the telephone. The public generally and the businessmen were slow to perceive any value in the telephone. The scientific world on the other hand took it up at once." Despite his grasp of the importance and utility of the telephone, Bell also shared the sentiments of many modern businesspeople who find the telephone simply irritating. One of Bell's servants at his summer home in Baddeck Bay, Nova Scotia, said that Bell would immediately stuff a towel around his own phone upon entering his lab to prevent anyone from interrupting him; "Now a man can think !" he would say.

At 6:25 P.M. on August 4, 1922, two days after Bell's death, all railway and telephone service in North America was suspended for one minute to mark his passing.

RADIO
First transatlantic wireless message

There were many dramatic episodes and personalities in the early days of radio in Canada. Guglielmo Marconi, famous pioneer in radio, though not Canadian, received the first transatlantic wireless message on a hilltop at St. John's, Newfoundland on Thursday, December 12, 1901. The transmission was sent from Poldhu in southwestern Cornwall, England. Marconi was seen as a direct threat to the Newfoundland cable companies whose stock began to plummet the following Monday. Instead of incorporating Marconi and his achievement into their own operations, they claimed exclusive rights to telegraph communications from the island and had Marconi kicked out of Newfoundland two weeks later. Nine-tenths of wisdom consists of being wise in time, according to an old saying, and it's easy to be sage as we look back. Newfoundland cable companies still may be kicking themselves, however, for this missed chance in the early days of Canadian radio.

The government of Canada quickly seized the opportunity and offered Marconi $80,000 to set up his wireless operations at Glace Bay, Cape Breton Island. The money was used to construct a wireless station connecting Canada to England and led to the establishment by federal charter of Canada's first electronics company, the Marconi Wireless Telegraph Co. of Canada Ltd., located in Montreal. It also began what is now a long tradition of government support for excellent quality in radio in Canada.

First wireless voice message

Only a year earlier, on December 23, 1900, radio inventor Reginald Aubrey Fessenden (1866-1932) had transmitted history's first wireless voice message. He applied his belief that sound traveled in continuous waves to an experiment on that day, on Cobb Island on the Potomac River near Washington, DC, when he transmitted his voice between two fifty-foot towers, one mile (1.61 kilometers) apart, asking his assistant, "Is it snowing where you are, Mr. Thiessen? If it is, telegraph back and let me know." The Quebec-born inventor, after working in Thomas A. Edison's laboratory in New Jersey in 1887, devoted himself to work on radio broadcasting. He worked for Westinghouse, the U.S. Weather Service and two U.S. universities before forming his own company in 1902. Fessenden discovered the superheterodyne principle, the basis of all modern broadcasting.

First radio voice broadcast

On December 24, 1906, Fessenden made the first radio voice broadcast to crews of ships in the Atlantic and Caribbean, performing carol singing, Bible reading and violin playing for them himself. He made the broadcast from the four hundred and twenty foot (one hundred and twenty-eight meter) radio mast of the National Electric Signalling Company at Brant Rock, Massachusetts. He lost control of the company in which he was a partner in 1910 when his partners forced him out. During World War I he gave the allied governments the right to use any of his inventions without compensation to him, and he was active in developing new devices for use by the military. At the same time, when his former partners sold the rights to many of his patents to the U.S Radio Trust without his permission, Fessenden sued the Trust for compensation for infringement of his patents. The lawsuits, at one time seeking total compensation of $60 million, dragged on for years, until finally, in 1928, the Radio Trust agreed to pay $2.5 million in an out of court settlement. The Institute of Radio Engineers gave Fessenden their Medal of Honor for out-standing achievement in radio technology, and the City of Philadelphia gave him the Scott Medal for work of great value to humanity. Fessenden also developed the fathometer, a device for measuring the depth of water. It won him the Scientific American Gold Medal.

First scheduled radio broadcast and first commercial radio station

The Marconi Wireless Telegraph Company of Canada set up station XWA in downtown Montreal in November 1918 for use in experiments and as an advertising device. Regular broadcasts began in December 1919 and on May 20, 1920, one of the first scheduled radio broadcasts in North America took place as XWA transmitted a musical program from Montreal to a meeting of the Royal Society of Canada in Ottawa. The XWA transmitter became the first transmitter for the CFCF station when it was set up as a commercial radio station on November 4, 1920, one of the first regular broadcasting stations in the world. Its call letters stand for "Canada's First, Canada's Finest." Marconi's company has been called the Canadian Marconi Company since 1925 and the major shareholder with 51.6 percent of outstanding shares is now the General Electric Company (GEC) of the United Kingdom. Other Marconi companies around the world are wholly owned by GEC. The Marconi Company is now an international leader in the design and production of military and commercial electronics products and systems.

First batteryless radio and radio station

Another Canadian first in radio came in April 1925, when Edward Samuel Rogers (1900-39) invented the world's first commercial alternating-current radio tube. Suddenly batteryless radio, the first radio that could be operated on normal household electric current, became a reality. In March, 1927, Rogers received a patent for the AC batteryless radio. Also in 1927, Rogers started the world's first all electric batteryless broadcasting station. Its call letters, CFRB, stand for the state of the art in radio at the time. CF is the once-standard broadcast prefix for "Canada" and RB stands for "Roger's Batteryless."

FOREMOST WIREPHOTO TRANSMITTER

The man called "Intrepid," Sir William Stephenson (1896-1989), had made a major development in the field of communications years before he achieved fame as chief of the British Security Co-ordination in New York during World War II. In 1921, Stephenson invented a new means of transmitting photographs by wireless that was much faster and better than earlier models. His new transmitter was first used in December 1922 and by 1924 he had perfected the device. The transmitter was eventually used by newspapers all over the world, and laid the ground work for the development of television, which transmits images in a similar fashion.

Stephenson worked out the theory of the transmitter in Canada, but the refinement and the actual construction of the first working model took place in England. He ended up a millionaire before he was thirty years old. In 1940, Stephenson was appointed Britain's chief espionage agent in North America, and remained in that position until 1945, when he was knighted for his services. He is known as "the Quiet Canadian" because of his secrecy about his military work.

TELESAT CANADA
First domestic geostationary communications satellite

On November 9,1972, Canada launched the world's first geostationary domestic communications satellite, Anik-1, from Cape Canaveral, Florida, establishing the world's first domestic communications satellite system. The process that led up to this launch began on May 2, 1969, when Telesat Canada was formed by an agreement between the Canadian federal government and Trans-Canada Telephone Systems. On August 30, 1970, Telesat Canada and Hughes Aircraft Company of California signed an agreement to build Anik-1.

Many firsts in the field of domestic telecommunications followed the launch of Anik-1. Canada broadcast the world's first national television system via satellite and today broadcasts a greater range of services than any other satellite network in the world. Television, radio, telephone, and data transmissions services are provided to homes and offices throughout Canada by the network.

Canada has maintained a commitment to improve national communication for its small population over its huge land mass, including developing national radio, film, a national corporation for public broadcasting as well as the satellite communications system. Telesat broadcasts educational information, pay television, and private television broadcasting, all in French and English. The arrangement allows information and programs to be exchanged and broadcast to remote areas of Canada. Anik channels are used by the Canadian Broadcasting Corporation to assemble and exchange program material from one city to another. Also, the satellite network carries live coverage of Canada's Parliament in session and made Canada one of the first nations to offer its citizens "teledemocracy" when broadcasts began on October 17, 1977. Finally, *The Globe and Mail*, Canada's major daily newspaper, is carried nationwide via satellite from Toronto to printing plants in Vancouver, Calgary, Brandon, Ottawa, and Moncton.

Telesat Canada is a commercial, shareholder-owned company, that depends on its commercial sales, and in which the federal government holds a large, but not majority, share. Its over twenty years of operational experience with telecommunications satellites has created great demand for its services in countries developing their own satellite systems.

BLISSYMBOLICS

Australian Charles K. Bliss originally invented Blissymbolics to be used as an international language. Shirley McNaughton discovered the system in 1971 when she was trying to develop a way to communicate with her students who have cerebral palsy. McNaughton and a multi-disciplinary team at the Ontario Crippled Children's Centre in Toronto (called the Hugh MacMillan Medical Centre since 1985) adapted the system for use by non-speaking people. The system is now used all over the world as Bliss intended, but mainly among people with cerebral palsy who cannot speak. In 1975, the Blissymbolics Communication Foundation was established to maintain standard symbol form and to provide information to the growing number of people who want to use the system.

To use Blissymbolics successfully, persons must first be assessed to determine the best way to meet their needs and to overcome their limitations. A Bliss board or display folder is set up for that person. There are fourteen thousand approved Blissymbols and each part of the symbol has a meaning assigned to it so it is possible to create new words by combining symbol parts. Students begin by using a pictographic system of symbols that look like that which they are meant to symbolize. They build up their vocabulary over time. To communicate, the user points to the symbols which have English translations above them. The system is effective because anyone who can read can understand what the Blissymbol user communicates. If users cannot point to the symbols with their hands, other methods, such as a pointer attached to their head, can be used. Computers are also used instead of a Bliss board by placing a template over the keyboard, and matching the Bliss symbols with the corresponding keys.

The communication that Blissymbolics makes possible has made a huge difference in the lives of people with cerebral palsy. Before learning how to communicate through Blissymbolics, students often had what were perceived to be behavioral problems and were labelled as being immature as a result of their frustration at not being able to communicate. Even some of the people who worked most closely with people with cerebral palsy were under the impression that they were not able to learn. However, once they learn how to communicate through Blissymbolics, people with cerebral palsy can learn how to read and operate a computer and can overcome their barriers of communication.

C N TOWER—
Tallest freestanding structure in the world

The tallest freestanding structure in the world stands as a landmark of Toronto and of Canada's commitment to telecommunications. Completed in 1975, the tower was constructed over almost two and one-half years by Canadian National Railways. It cost $52 million to build and stands 1,815 feet and 5 inches high (553.34 meters). Every year the tower attracts almost two million visitors who take the tour of the broadcasting facilities or visit the observation deck and the world's highest revolving restaurant. The tower is owned by Canadian National (CN), a Crown (government) corporation. The government of Canada is the sole owner of the corporation.

The CN Tower has greatly extended the range of the television and radio stations that use the tower to broadcast their signals. Before the construction of the tower, the skyscrapers of downtown Toronto blocked shorter radio and television signals. Now smaller antennas are able to broadcast to the tower and have their signal relayed over a wide area. The Canadian Broadcasting Company (CBC), CN Canada and CFNY radio station have recording studios in the tower and approximately twenty other broadcasting stations use the tower as a relaying base.

Medicine

S IR WILLIAM OSLER—
Father of Psychosomatic Medicine

Called the father of psychosomatic medicine, Sir William Osler (1849-1919) developed a unique philosophy behind his practice of medicine. Combining physiological and psychological treatments, Osler's philosophy is reflected in such success stories as Norman Cousin's battle with a disease of the connective tissue through laughter. Given to practical jokes and a vivacious manner that instilled patients with hope, Osler believed that the patient's state of mind was of ultimate importance in his or her cure. He is famous for describing the failure of the medical school curriculum to cultivate this attitude, and his efforts resulted in changes that remain to this day, particularly a decrease in the time medical students spend in the classroom and an increase in the time they spend with patients.

Born at Bond Head, Ontario, on July 12, 1849, Osler graduated in medicine from McGill University in Montreal in 1872. He continued his studies in Europe for two years before returning to McGill to teach physiology and pathology. Osler subsequently taught at University of Pennsylvania (from 1884); he was the first professor of medicine at John Hopkins University in Baltimore (from 1889) and from 1905 to his death he occupied the Regius Chair of Medicine at Oxford University. At the turn of the century he was probably the best known physician in the English-speaking world and he has also been called "the most influential physician in history", both for his bedside manner and his inspirational speeches. While some Canadians found that their inventions left them laughing all the way to the bank, Osler's innovations left him and many of his followers simply laughing.

H OSPITAL FOR SICK CHILDREN—
Pioneering work in the treatment of sick children

The Hospital for Sick Children (HSC) was started in the spring of 1875 by a group of Toronto women organized by Elizabeth McMaster. It was the first Canadian hospital devoted exclusively to "admission and treatment of all sick children regardless of creed and colour." Known as Sick Kids, the HSC cares for 280,000 patients annually and is recommended internationally as one of the best in children's care. At the same time it conducts extensive research into childhood diseases at its Research Institute, which has 587 beds and is one of the largest pediatric research institutes in the world. Hundreds of research projects on a wide range of problems, from the common bronchial cold to brain disorders, are ongoing at the HSC every year.

Through past investigations into children's health, the hospital has discovered many important treatment techniques. Major steps have been made at Sick Kids in the treatment and diagnosis of cystic fibrosis and the diagnosis of muscular dystrophy. The hospital has perfected the "blue baby operation", which involves the transposition of the great vessels of the heart, saving countless infant lives. It pioneered a surgical procedure to correct congenital dislocation of the hip, allowing children with this problem to walk and live normally. It pioneered two major corrective procedures for scoliosis: the spinal pacemaker system and Super Stability Fusion (SSF) surgery.

D ISCOVERY OF INSULIN

Many people take it for granted that diabetes can be easily controlled with daily shots of insulin and careful eating. But in 1921, more than one million people in North America had diabetes, and there was nothing anyone could do for them. They wasted away on a starvation diet that might have helped them last a little longer, while suffering from gangrene and other degenerating symptoms. No one knew what caused the disease or how to treat it.

Then, a dogged young man, Frederick Banting (1891-1941), inspired to become a doctor after witnessing a doctor save a man's life at the site of an accident, discovered insulin and its value for the diabetic. Banting was twenty-nine at the time he made the discovery with his student, Charles H. Best, at the University of Toronto. Banting always described himself and his part in the discovery as a catalyst, an agent that promotes a reaction without taking part in it. Others took different view of Banting's role in the discovery, and he was awarded the Nobel Prize for Physiology or Medicine in 1923 and later was knighted for his achievement. He was quite upset that Best was not recognized as co-discoverer. Instead the head of Banting's department at the university, J.J.R. MacLeod (1876-1935), who had supervised the research project, was named to share the prize. In the end, Banting shared his monetary reward with Best (1899-1978) and Macleod shared his with J.B. Collip (1892-1965), who had also been involved in the discovery. Banting did not take out a patent on insulin but instead turned over the rights to the University of Toronto, and the patent rights for the manufacture of insulin were assigned to Medical Research Council of Canada. The substance was made available by late 1922.

Ask any Canadian to name things their country has done first or does better than the United States, and quite justifiably Banting's discovery is often the first thing they mention. The miraculous role insulin plays in so many people's lives today is testimony to the importance of Banting's achievement, and it remains a landmark in the history of medical research in Canada.

HANS SELYE— ## Pioneer in Stress-Disease Links

It is commonly accepted that Hans Selye (1907-82) opened up new vistas in the study of man's relationship with his environment and in the view of adaptations of a living organism to change. His legacy has provided fuel for controversy and theories being explored in this age of molecular biology and neurochemistry. Born in Vienna in 1907, Selye studied in Prague, Paris, and Rome before he was awarded the Rockefeller Research Fellowship to work at John Hopkins University in Baltimore in 1931. In 1932, he moved to the department of Biochemistry at McGill University in Montreal. From McGill, Selye joined the faculty at the Université de Montreal in 1945, where he stayed until 1976. That year Selye founded the International Institute of Stress in Montreal of which he was president until his death in 1982.

Selye's aim in most of his work, which began in 1936, was to show the link between diseases and stress and adaptation to stress. He maintained that reactions through pituitary and adrenal activity are the central feature of adaptation. The concept of stress being a part of the defense system against disease was conceived and evolved by Selye. He is best known for establishing the link between psychological stress and biochemical changes in the body and the discovery of catatoxic steroids and their role in the body's defense mechanisms. At a time when the study of endocrinology (the study of glands that regulate certain body functions) was expanding rapidly, Selye's theory aroused considerable interest. Colleagues wondered how a gland as tiny as the pituitary, tucked away at the base of the brain, could become aware of stress while controlling the activity of the other endocrine glands. This question fascinated two of Selye's most promising students, Doctors Claude Fortier and Roger Guillemin. Guillemin received the Nobel Prize for his work in this field in 1977.

Selye had a wide-ranging mind with a special ability to synthesize information from diverse fields. He liked to propose hypotheses on a broad scale, while leaving the verifications and applications in other fields to the clinicians. While some might have criticized him for this, others knew that it is often the "silly" question (or hypothesis) that leads to a totally new development. Notions that Selye put forward based on experience with animals were generalized beyond the laboratory and formed the basis of explanations for some behavioral disturbances in humans. In this way, Selye arrived at the concepts of the general adaptation syndrome, the equilibrium of hormonal secretions during adaptation, hormonal tension as a cause of disease, and of catatoxic hormones. His connection of aging, schizophrenia, and cardiovascular disease to the adrenal gland and his studies of hypertension as it relates to hormone overreproduction and arthritis opened new doors in the exploration of how the body reacts to stress.

Dr. Selye authored more than fourteen hundred publications in technical journals, as well as twenty-six books. He was awarded many honorary degrees in many countries; he was a fellow of the Royal Society of Canada and was made a Companion of the Order of Canada, the country's highest honor. He was also a brilliant educator who trained leading researchers.

WILDER GRAVES PENFIELD—
Canada's Foremost Neurologist

Wilder Graves Penfield (1891-1976), a neurosurgeon and scientist, was born in Spokane, Washington in 1891. Though he received most of his formal schooling in the United States, the greatest influence on his work was Sir William Osler, whom he met during a stint at Merton College in Oxford in 1913. In 1928, Penfield moved to work at Montreal's Royal Victoria Hospital. Penfield's most enduring contribution there has turned out to be founding the now world famous Montreal Neurological Institute in 1934. He served as its director until 1960.

At the Institute, epilepsy became Penfield's great teacher in his exploration of the workings of the brain. Some of the modern theories of the separate functions of the two cerebral hemispheres were founded upon discoveries he made doing research on seizures. Penfield considered neurology to be the most unexplored frontier in science. Of it he wrote: "The problem of neurology is to understand man himself." His early studies of epilepsy encouraged Penfield to undertake a systematic mapping of the brain. This work was continued at the Institute. Consisting of a neurological hospital and a brain research center, the Institute continues to have international impact. The cooperation of both basic scientists and physicians at the Institute has served as a model for similar units throughout the world.

Dr. Penfield received the the Order of Merit in 1953 and in 1958 the French Médaille Lannelongue. In 1959, he was made a member of the Soviet Academy of Sciences, one of the first two Canadians to be so honored, along with Dr. Edgar William Richard Steacie (1900-62), once chair of the National Research Council. In 1967, Penfield was awarded the first Royal Bank fifty thousand dollar prize and Centennial Medal and was one of the first group of Canadians to be named a Companion of the Order of Canada, the country's highest honor.

NORMAN BETHUNE

Norman Bethune (1890-1939) was born in the small Ontario town of Gravenhurst. He died a hero forty-nine years later in a one-room house in north China. During his life he served the wounded in three wars and made his mark on three continents. He served as a stretcher bearer in a field ambulance unit with the Canadian army in France in 1915; he went to fight fascism in Spain in 1936, and by 1938 he had left for China to aid the Chinese in their fight against the Japanese.

Bethune came from a line of physicians, clergymen, fur traders and businessmen. His father was an evangelical Presbyterian minister. Bethune chose to become a surgeon, like his grandfather, the first Dr. Norman Bethune. Bethune's experience with tuberculosis in both lungs, led to a revision of his professional goals during an intensely introspective period as he was recovering in a sanatorium. At first he put his energies into exploring new techniques in thoracic surgery for victims of tuberculosis, at times testing some of his theories on himself. In 1928, he joined Dr. Edward Archibald's surgical team at Montreal's Royal Victoria Hospital.

Bethune's eight years in Montreal were critical ones, professionally, personally, and politically. He produced over a dozen medical instruments, and was widely published in professional journals. He also provoked substantial criticism. His creativity extended to painting, poetry, and prose, and a remarriage and redivorce to and from his wife Frances, an upper middle-class Edinburgh woman. His eventual disillusionment with medicine came as a result of an increased awareness that patients whose disease had been arrested by surgery too often became ill once again after returning to the squalid conditions that caused their original problems. He perceived society as being sick, and after soul-searching and a visit to the Soviet Union, Bethune secretly joined the Communist Party in late 1935. During this time he introduced a health clinic for unemployed persons in Montreal and challenged his profession to promote reform in medical care and health systems.

First mobile blood-transfusion service and first mobile medical unit

Bethune's work in Montreal was interrupted by the outbreak of the Spanish Civil War in 1936. While working for the Loyalists in Madrid, he revolutionized battlefield medical care by organizing the world's first mobile blood-transfusion service. In 1938, Bethune left for China. Serving as Mao Zedong's Army Medical Chief in the Eighth Route Army in the northern hills of Yenan, Bethune trained medics and doctors from the people in the army. It was in this rugged countryside that the Chinese people came to know Norman Bethune. During his short stay Bethune was to overcome the hard, barren hills, the poverty of the people and the absence of antibiotics and proper surgical instruments. Bethune brought with him the latest scientific knowledge and experience in war surgery. He understood the importance of immediate surgery for the wounded, the need to control shock, bleeding, pain, and more. His efforts were dedicated to teaching, traveling, and operating where he was needed. He formed the world's first mobile medical unit, which could be carried on two mules, to facilitate his work. For the lack of a few grams of penicillin, Bethune died of complications caused by an infected wound he suffered while operating, as usual, without surgical gloves.

Ten years later, the People's Republic of China formed, an essay by Mao Zedong was published that extolled Bethune's "boundless sense of responsibility" and held him up as a lesson in internationalism for the Chinese people, internationalism that was both against narrow nationalism and narrow patriotism. Bethune became a leading hero and martyr for the Chinese people, second only to Mao. The Chinese call him "Pai-ch'iu-en", which means White Seeks Grace. He was originally buried at Chu-ch'eng in 1940 under the Chinese and American flags because a Union Jack could not be found. His body was exhumed and reburied at Shih-chia Chuang, in northern China, in 1952 and close by his tomb are a larger-than-life statue, a pavilion, a museum, and the Norman Bethune International Peace Hospital, all dedicated to Bethune. The family home in Gravenhurst is now a museum, and on August 17, 1972, the federal government declared Dr. Bethune a Canadian of national historic significance and unveiled a plaque in Gravenhurst. On August 30, 1976, a delegation of seventeen Chinese government officials attended the official opening of the restored birthplace of Bethune.

The Chinese also donated a statue of Bethune that stands in downtown Montreal.

B REAKTHROUGHS IN CANCER TREATMENT

The cobalt "bomb"

Canada was the first country to develop a radiation source stronger than the X-ray to treat cancer patients. W.V. Mayneard, head of the physics department of the Royal Canadian Hospital in England, in conversation with two of his colleagues, J.S. Mitchell and J.V. Dunforth, discussed the idea in 1945 that the radioactive isotope cobalt-60 could possibly be used for cancer treatment. However, at that time cobalt-60 of the appropriate specific activity was not yet available.

In 1951, Canada produced two batches of radioactive cobalt-60 of the appropriate specific activity from the Chalk River nuclear plant, four years before any other country could do so. That same year, the first Cobalt "bomb" therapy unit, designed by scientists at Eldorado Nuclear, was established at London, Ontario in a clinic of the Ontario Cancer Foundation and the first treatment was given there on October 27, 1951. Another unit, designed by Dr. H. E. Johns, was set up shortly afterwards at the University of Saskatchewan. He designed the head to regulate the amount of radiation received by the patient and to protect those administering the therapy. The live cobalt was placed within thick walls of lead with the opening pointed at an indelible target painted on the patient's skin. The beam of radiation concentrated on the tumor, ionizing cancerous cells and inhibiting their growth. As a result, healthy cells have a chance to repair the damage that has been done. The Canadian units became models for treatment machines around the world, replacing X-ray treatment of many cancers. Cobalt is still widely used for diagnostic and therapeutic purposes (mainly cancer treatment) and Canada has continued to lead the world in the development of the treatment units.

The carcino embryonic antigen (CEA) test

Discovered in 1968 by Dr. Phil Gold and colleagues when he was a Ph.D. student in cancer and immunology research in Montreal, the CEA test is the blood test most often used for cancer. Since 1980, Gold has been the physician-in-chief at the Montreal General Hospital, where he oversees the department of medicine; has turned the cancer center into one of the best in North America; and established an AIDS laboratory in 1982, one of the first in Canada. But back in 1963, Gold was a twenty-seven-year-old Ph.D. student with funding for two years' work under Dr. Samuel Freedman, then head of immunology at the General. His work was focused on the search for "tumor markers", or antigens, molecular proteins in or on cancer cells which the immune system reacts to because of their different chemical makeup from healthy tissue. After a series of experiments Gold demonstrated the existence of the first identifiable tumor antigen. He then located the appearance of the antigen, finding it in all cancers of the digestive tract, and in fetuses between the third and sixth months of gestation, after which it disappears. From this discovery came the name for the antigen.

Between 1966 and 1968, Gold and his colleagues studied CEA, and found that it is a large molecule made up mainly of carbohydrates and protein, and that it is located on the outside coat of the cancer cell. Gold followed a hunch and with a few more tests was able to show that CEA moved off the cancer cells and into the bloodstream of cancer patients. He announced the test results in 1970, and the medical world soon realized that the first blood test for cancer had been discovered.

Since Gold's discovery, it has been shown that a small proportion of people test positive for CEA, even though they have diseases other than cancers of the digestive tract. This has meant that the test cannot be used as a simple screen for bowel cancer, as first hoped. However, the test is used extensively to monitor the progress of patients after surgery, to see whether the removal of a tumor has been successful. In 1982, Gold won the first Manning Principal Award (for Canadian innovations) for his development of the test.

Now researchers are working to increase the specificity of the CEA test. Working under Gold's supervision at the General, Abraham Fuks, a specialist in monoclonal antibodies, and Clifford Stanners, a molecular geneticist, have cloned a gene for CEA, duplicated its genetic code, and produced synthetic versions of the antigen.

F IRSTS IN MYOELECTRIC PROSTHESES

Canadians have made definite, outstanding contributions to the development of "myoelectric" prostheses, especially for children, and in some ways are world leaders in the field today. Canada's participation began in the early 1960s when Dr. Gustave Gingras of the Rehabilitation Institute of Montreal paid twenty-seven thousand dollars for the rights to produce a myoelectric control system brought from England. The original system had been developed by the Soviet Union solely for use by adult males. It was produced commercially by a company in Vienna. Dr. Gingras ran a project at the Institute to design a control system of its own, adaptable to women and children. The system involves miniaturized components and internal wiring that control the prosthesis according to the amount of muscular electrical stimulation. Surface electrodes in the system are attached to muscles and pick up the electrical signal released when the muscle contracts. The first patient was fitted in 1965 with a system that controlled a hook.

First commercially produced electric hand for children

At the time, Dr. Gingras realized that the system did not solve all the problems for patients, or necessarily replace conventional devices, and because of the diverse nature of patients' problems, he doubted that a standard device could be developed to serve all cases. However, Canada has a program unique in the world to overcome this apparent limitation. It began with the first myoelectric fitting of a hook on a twelve-year-old boy in Canada at the Ontario Crippled Children's Centre (now called the Hugh MacMillan Rehabilitation Centre). In 1971, at the Centre, Helmut Lukas developed the first electrically powered child-size hand in the world. The hand was first fitted to a patient by William F. Sauter at the Centre. It was then marketed by Variety Village Electro-Limb Production Centre (now called VASI—Variety Abilities Systems Incorporated, a manufacturer and distributor of myoelectric hands), becoming the first commercially produced child's hand in the world, exported to Spain, Sweden, England, and the United States.

The Centre is the only organization in the world to specialize in developing myoelectric arms, elbows and hands for children. Its unique development program is based on a connection with Variety Village: Dr. Milner, head of Rehabilitation Engineering at the Centre, also heads up Variety Village. This allows the Centre to work on a clinical and practical level and get results unmatched in the world. The clinical and prototype teams work at the Centre; the physicians, therapists, and prosthetic specialists work with the patients; and design engineers and tool and dye makers work in a prototype mechanics shop to produce a prototype of the prosthesis according to the specifications of the clinical team. After the prototype has been tested, evaluated and proven its worth, it is sent to Variety Village for small scale commercial production, fifty to one hundred units at a time. The limbs are sold all over the world on a nonprofit basis.

Most children fitted in the world

Using this process, the Centre has produced a whole range of child's hands to fit children from fifteen to eighteen months old through their teens. They have also developed three types of electric elbows. The standard-size hands and elbows are fitted to each individual patient using a molded, custom-made prosthesis called a socket. The Centre has fitted more children than any other organization in the world. It has sixty children on its active file who were fitted before they were six years old; its oldest patient is sixty-eight years old, its youngest, sixteen months.

In March of 1987, the Hugh MacMillan Rehabilitation Centre completed the fitting of two complete myoelectric arms with hands for Steve Simonar, of Saskatoon, Saskatchewan. According to William Sauter, Mr. Simonar was fitted with the most sophisticated prostheses in the world ever developed and fitted to a person. The arms have electric elbows used as shoulder joints and are controlled by means of switches located at the shoulder and on Mr. Simonar's chest. The shoulders are "abduction joints" meaning that they only move along one plane and cannot rotate at different angles. However, Mr. Simonar's arms have humeral rotators at the elbow joints which allow rotation and they also have wrist rotators. The hands have a pinch power between the thumb and forefinger twenty-five to fifty percent greater than that of the average person.

Since 1987, the Centre has continued its work developing hands and elbows for persons of various ages. The Centre also developed and fitted an electric "orthosis" brace. This was added on to an existing limb that was paralyzed in order to support it and allow movement of the elbow and hand myoelectrically by very small muscle movements of the eyebrows which were hooked into electrodes installed in a pair of eyeglasses.

Education and
Social Welfare

F IRST Y.M.C.A.
IN NORTH AMERICA

In 1847, two young evangelical businessmen, Francis
Grafton and James Clexton, returned from England with the charter
of the Y.M.C.A. that they had received from the association's founder,
Sir George Williams. Both men were concerned with the community
welfare of Montreal. Because of Montreal's mixed population, as
opposed to the Roman Catholic dominated Quebec City, they felt that
it would be possible to make some progress in evangelical work
there. After nearly four years of work in Montreal, they were able to
establish the first North American chapter of the Young Men's
Christian Association there on November 25, 1851, just one month
before a Y.M.C.A. chapter was formed in Boston, Massachusetts.

The symbol for the Y.M.C.A., one triangle within another,
represents the three areas of spirit, mind and body that the Association tries to improve. The triangle within the other represents a
person within their community. At different times during its history,
the Montreal Y.M.C.A. has emphasized different parts of the trio. At
the beginning, the Christian aspect of the Y.M.C.A. (Y) was emphasized. Then sport became the focus. Then, in 1870, the Association
started up night adult education classes for people who worked
during the day but wanted to complete their education. People were
so enthusiastic about the program that in 1926 the Y founded Sir
George Williams College, now part of Concordia University.

In the 1950s, the Christian aspect of the Y was replaced
by a more general emphasis on human values. The Y continues to

fulfill its community role by protecting minority rights, promoting the creation of enterprises for young kids having problems with drugs and delinquency, and helping to get local residents hired by businesses in the area. The Y is unique in that it is completely bilingual, and this allows it to help both English and French youngsters understand and adjust to each other's culture. Because its emphasis is on contributing to the personal growth of the youth of Montreal, the Y also contributes to the leadership and long-term development of the entire community.

F RONTIER COLLEGE—
Foremost in Adult Education

Frontier College is a voluntary organization founded in Toronto in 1899 as the Reading Camp Association by Alfred Fitzpatrick, a Presbyterian minister from Nova Scotia. Educator E.W. Bradwin joined the organization as an instructor in 1904 and became Fitzpatrick's deputy. Incorporated in 1922 by an act of Parliament, the College examined the problem of illiteracy, not widely recognized at the time, in an unusual and creative way. During the summer months, young people educated in colleges and universities volunteered to work in isolated mining, lumber, and railway camps in many areas of Canada. Working during the day with the crews, at night the students would hold school classes in basic subjects for their fellow workers. Through correspondence courses and the field teachers, Frontier College provides educational opportunities for workers who would not have them otherwise.

Fitzpatrick expressed the premise of the College as this; "Wherever and whenever people have occasion to congregate, then and there should be the time, place and means of education." His intent was to provide educational opportunities to people ranging from basic education through degree-granting programs. In 1932, the College reduced its original range of instruction to concentrate on adult basic education. At this time, the act that had incorporated the College was amended removing the College's authority to grant degrees. The College had granted only six degrees in the ten-year period since it had been federally chartered. Another reason for this change was that education is regulated provincially in Canada and the College's federal status conflicted with this administrative structure. In 1936, Bradwin became the second Principal of the College.

Frontier College focuses on the energy of young Canadians in building valuable human resources in their own country. In 1977, Frontier College won the United Nations Education, Scientific, and Cultural Organization (UNESCO) prize for achievement in adult literacy. Dr. Wendell Macleod, a contemporary of Norman Bethune who participated in the program in his youth, said he learned as much or more from the people he worked with as he taught them. Education at Frontier College works both for the teacher and the student. Their philosophy, "Tell me and I'll forget; show me I may remember; but involve me and I'll understand," stresses this relationship.

Today, the laborer/teacher program continues in rail gangs and in power plants. The teachers receive laborer's pay from their employers and a stipend from the College. Teaching is still flexible and based on what the students want to learn, from basic reading and math skills to describing and opening doors to further education. The College's literacy programs have expanded to include courses in which students and parents tutor each other, tutors work with street kids, native people in Vancouver tutor each other, and volunteer tutors work in prisons. A musical show also tours, giving lessons and free books to kids. Program funding comes from private charitable donations, government grants and service contracts. Frontier College has persisted with its belief that everyone deserves a chance to learn according to their desire to learn, an idea that has comes into its own.

OLDEST ENGLISH DAY-CARE CENTER IN NORTH AMERICA

The Montreal Day Nursery, which celebrated its hundredth anniversary in 1988, is believed to be the oldest English daycare center in North America. It began in a cramped room with six children who were taken care of by a mother who had two children of her own. Since then, the Nursery, which was incorporated in 1900, moved several times before settling into its present location at the Drummond St. Y.M.C.A. in Montreal. It has been funded over the years by a variety of sources, from the fundraising activities of a committee of twelve women recruited in the early days by a certain Rev. Dr. Barnes, to the Red Feather organization, which funded it from 1922 to 1976, to its current funders: parents and Quebec's Department of Social Affairs mainly, and in part the Montreal Day Nursery Foundation.

C REDIT UNIONS

The first credit union in North America was founded at Lévis, Quebec, on December 16, 1900, by Alphonse Desjardins (1854-1920). Called La Caisse Populaire de Lévis (The People's Bank of Lévis), it opened for business on January 23, 1901. In 1906, Desjardins came to the United States to help establish the first credit union, in New Hampshire. Today, Canada has approximately 3,400 and the United States approximately 16,500 established credit unions. In Canada one-third of the population belongs to a credit union; in some rural areas there are no banks, and people rely solely on credit unions for all their financial needs. In the United States, about fifty-six million people are members of credit unions and the hundred largest credit unions are spread over twenty-five states, many in the southern rural states.

Desjardins was a journalist from a poor farm family and had experienced and witnessed the lack of banking facilities appropriate to the common wage earner. While covering the House of Commons in Ottawa, he reported on testimony and debates on a bill to outlaw usury, hearing one man speak of having to pay 1,200 percent interest on a modest loan. Having heard of the development of the cooperative credit movement in Europe, he decided to explore the possibility of similar cooperatives in Canada. Convinced that "the local circumstances are of such a character as to completely warrant me to go into the enterprise with the conviction that it will confer a great benefit on the people, who, being not in a position to go to our ordinary Banks, are obliged to subscribe to the terrible conditions imposed on them by private money lenders," Desjardins established a credit union. As they became popular, credit unions provided competition for the banks, causing them to revise some of their exploitative practices in areas such as interest rates, mortgages and administrative costs. The credit unions also developed innovations that the banks readily copied, such as convenient service hours.

During the first six years, the Lévis credit union made loans totalling two hundred thousand dollars and did not lose one cent, proving that the cooperative principle provided necessary security. As Desjardins said then, "The main security is the fact that the association is working within a small area and that everybody knows each other, a second security is that everybody is interested by being a shareholder." This statement still characterizes credit unions.

Today, credit unions in both the United States and Canada must be approved by the government, and are regularly inspected. They are still generally small (in the U.S. eighty percent of the credit unions have less than five million dollars each in assets), but in 1986 in the U.S. they held $183 billion in assets in total. And credit unions still offer the advantage of greater independence and better service for people who otherwise might have to depend on large private financial institutions. In a 1986 *American Banker* survey, sixty-four percent of those naming a credit union as their principal financial institution said they were "very satisfied" with their credit union, compared to fifty-six percent for thrift customers and fifty-four percent for commercial bank customers. As Desjardins explained in 1907 to a Special Committee of the House of Commons, "Now when you get down to the details of it, one of the great advantages of cooperation is that it teaches people how to do their own business instead of relying on a middleman. . . . You will find it has taught people the great advantages of economy, thrift, saving, and above all, it has taught them the value of the cents, the small savings."

COOPERATIVES

Cooperatives have been able to develop in Canada to a much greater extent than in the United States. This is primarily because in the United States cooperatives cannot borrow money from credit unions, whereas in Canada such loans are a major factor in the expansion of both credit unions and cooperatives. The direct charge form of cooperative initiated in British Columbia is an example of how Canada has facilitated that expansion. Instituted in a supermarket or retail cooperative, the direct charge means that members are required to provide a much higher amount of initial capital to join the cooperative. A monthly membership charge of one to three dollars covers the fixed costs of operation, and items are priced to cover the variable costs of operation. Members pay for the operation of the cooperative whether or not they actually buy goods, so they tend to use it more. Although very successful in Canada, direct charge cooperatives have not formed in the United States due to lack of available capital and a membership base and the lack of wholesalers who might want to sponsor cooperatives.

The government of Canada has worked to facilitate the development of cooperatives, through providing financial support for the wheat pools during the Depression and in other ways. All cooperatives must be registered by the government, and they are frequently consolidated by this formal administration. The U.S. government, in contrast, has no department for the promotion and development of cooperatives, though it regulates them.

U.S. innovations in the cooperative movement have been adopted and developed to an even greater extent in Canada. A good example is the cooperative pooling of grain by grain growers that began in the U.S. Today, eighty-five percent of the Canadian grain that is exported is marketed through cooperatives. Canada has also been able to develop cooperative housing in a step-by-step manner. Again, the federal government worked with credit unions and provincial governments to create an infra-structure for a system of cooperative housing.

Another potent force in the development of cooperatives in Canada was a man by the name of Moses Coady. Born in Margaree, Nova Scotia, in 1882, Coady was an integral part of the Antigonish movement that developed in the late 1920s in Nova Scotia as an attempt to move the region towards self-sufficiency. Through educational and self-help campaigns, the movement pushed forward the ideas of cooperatives and credit unions as a means for people to take control of the local economy and become, as Coady's popular book was called, *Masters of Their Own Destiny*. The book was published in 1939, has been translated into seven languages, and is still in print. Coady's ultimate dream was to establish an international institute for the development of cooperatives. He died in 1959, his dream unrealized, but a few months later the Coady Institute was established at St. Francis Xavier University in Antigonish, Nova Scotia. The Institute was a pioneer in the development of cooperatives and in the 1960s educated through its programs many of the "fathers and mothers" of co-op movements in many other countries. Now the Institute's primary focus is to strengthen the existing people's organizations in countries in the developing world, and its work has expanded beyond promoting cooperatives and credit unions to exploring other means of organizing people to take control of the local economy. In 1989, the Institute had sixty-five students from twenty-seven countries enrolled in its course programs.

CANADIAN HEALTH-CARE SYSTEM

Although the current Canadian health care system is complex, at its core it is a government-run, nonprofit insurance plan that uses public funds to pay for a private, comprehensive system. Patients have free choice of physicians who are paid by separate provincial medical insurance plans on a fee-for-service basis. The federal government sponsors and administers the cost-sharing program with the provinces; in some provinces, the public is charged minimal premiums as subscribers to the services. The medical profession remains independent and self-regulating, and doctors are given the choice of opting in or out of the plan, according to their interests. Hospitals are not government owned, but locally controlled, nonprofit organizations.

The concept of universality (the service is available to all Canadians, regardless of income) with regard to health care and other social service programs is very important in Canada and is considered to be a "sacred trust" by some provincial governments. In contrast, in the United States forty million people are without any health insurance, more people than the entire population of Canada.

The Canadian health-care system grew out of successful voluntary medical service prepayment plans in several provinces. At a 1945 federal provincial conference, the federal government made an offer to underwrite sixty percent of the estimated costs of provincial medical, hospital, dental, pharmaceutical and nursing benefit programs, though it did not follow up on its offer because several provinces were opposed to the idea. In 1946, leading the rest of the provinces, Saskatchewan introduced the first program that set the basis for universal health insurance in Canada, dividing the province into fourteen health regions. Health Region No. 1, based in Swift

Current, established a district-wide medical insurance program that was Canada's first, partly funded by a special tax collected in the region, and partly funded by the government.

In 1956, the federal government offered to pay about half the costs of inpatient and outpatient hospitals, and, in 1957, to set up a federal payment formula whereby costs would be shared by various institutions and services. By 1961, all provincial governments had entered the hospital insurance scheme. Saskatchewan again led the other provinces in urging the federal government to expand its insurance coverage to physician services. The province's own "Medicare" plan, which covered physician's services, officially came into effect on July 1, 1962, and was implemented on August 2, 1962, when a special session of the Legislature passed amendments to the original Act to resolve a conflict between physicians and the government. Ninety percent of the physicians in the province had gone on strike and withdrawn their services when the government's legislation came into effect on July 1. In response, the federal government appointed the Royal Commission on Health Services (the Hall Commission) and six years later, on July 1, 1968, the Medical Care Act (Medicare) came into effect, establishing the present system which embodies four basic principles — universal coverage, comprehensive benefits, portability of benefits and public administration and accountability.

Today, the rising cost of providing universal health care is seen by some as a major, critical problem. The federal government re-worked the funding formula in 1977 and since then the provinces have shouldered a steadily increasing share of health costs. As well, the debate continues over whether physicians should be allowed to "extra bill" patients over and above the fees paid to them by Medicare. Canada's health care system is looked upon by the U.S. as a prime testing ground where many of the basic issues of services and costs are being joined. To date, Canada's expenditures have been in line with European countries at about 9.3 percent of its gross domestic product and well below the U.S., which has the most expensive medical system in the world accounting for 13 percent of gross domestic output. Despite the spending gap, Canada's system has produced lower infant mortality rates and longer life expectancy than the U.S.

Canadians are also pioneers in advocating a beyond-health-care system, which many see as a solution to the worries about the increasing costs of health care, as opposed to simply cutting services, privatizing the system, or both. Dr. Trevor Hancock of Toronto is a leading advocate of effective prevention of illness and maintenance of our health (health care) rather than effective treatment when we become ill (sick care). This implies that all areas of life and lifestyle and the environment must be improved in order to improve the health of the population. Health promotion, community health centers, preventive medicine programs and programs that improve the economic status and social and physical environments of Canadians are all seen as less expensive alternatives to the high-tech acute care that now dominates Canada's medical system. As Dr. Hancock has said, "A rational plan for a healthy future would see a society that would determine the major causes of disease and death, assess the factors leading to those causes, and then develop a deliberate and coherent set of public policies intended to create a healthy society."

VOTER REGISTRATION AND ELECTION FINANCING

Ever since Canada first came into existence as a nation, in 1867, the practice of government taking full responsibility for voter registration for elections has been in effect. A well-established tradition by now, the voter registration system in Canada has proven its worth by its success. In each election, whether federal, provincial or municipal, a door-to-door enumeration is conducted to get names of all eligible voters for the voter lists. At each level the process is similar. In federal elections, for example, the enumeration begins with the appointment of Chief Returning Officers (CROs) for each electoral district, or "riding." The CROs are responsible for appointing two enumerators for each polling station in their district (one per polling station in rural areas). The appointments are made in consultation with the political parties that have candidates in that district.

Enumerators must live in the district and be at least eighteen years old. They are paid on a per name basis with a minimum of two hundred names; forty cents for the first two hundred names, then sixty cents for every name after the first two hundred. The lists are compiled over a two week period and then checked and revised over another two weeks and completed two weeks before the election takes place. As more and more families have two working parents, Elections Canada has been using the mass media to a greater extent in order to reach people and make them aware of voter registration procedures. Using this system, Canada registers about 90 percent of the eligible voters for each election. In 1984, 98 percent of the eligible voters were registered for the federal election, a total of 16.3 million people. The almost universal registration has a marked effect on voter participation in Canada. Usually, over 70 percent of the registered voters cast their ballot—in 1984, 76.3 percent did so, and in 1988, 76 percent of registered voters participated in the federal elections. The lowest turnout since Confederation was 61 percent in 1896, and in thirty-four federal elections the turnout was less than 70 percent only five times. Voter turnout in federal elections has been 80 percent or higher five times.

Another notable part of Canada's election procedures is campaign financing. All of the provinces regulate campaign financing in some way. Financing for political campaigns is regulated by the Canada Elections Act. Spending limits for both candidates and political parties are tied to the number of registered voters. Candidates and parties receive an average of thirty cents per voter from the government for campaign expenses—the candidates for each voter registered in their riding, and the parties for each registered voter in ridings in which they have candidates. The thirty cents average per voter funding system was put in place in 1974 and since 1983 has been adjusted to reflect changes in the Consumer Price Index. The actual funding scale is one dollar for each of the first fifteen thousand voters, fifty cents per voter for the next ten thousand voters, and twenty-five cents per voter over twenty-five thousand voters. In 1984, the average amount received by candidates through this system was $50,000. The maximum amount that a party could receive in 1984, if it had candidates all two hundred eighty-two ridings, was $6.3 million. In 1988, with more voters in an additional thirteen new ridings and the Consumer Price Index adjustment, the maximum amount increased to just over $8 million.

Parties that spend more than 10 percent of the maximum amount get 22.5 percent of their election expenses paid for by Elections Canada. Each candidate who receives at least 15 percent of the vote gets half of his or her election expenses paid by Elections Canada. In addition, the source of individual donations to candidates or parties of more than $100 must be disclosed. However, in order to receive these benefits of the Canada Elections Act, a party must nominate at least fifty candidates in the election or have representation in the House of Commons when it dissolves for an election. All candidates and parties, however, must submit an audit of their campaign finances after the election to confirm that they have complied with election regulations.

Spending limitations for parties and candidates during elections have not been questioned for constitutionality in Canada as they have been in the United States. However, restrictions on so-called "third party spending" have been a main issue since 1983. In December 1983, the federal government passed a law that prohibited any person other than a candidate, official agent, or registered political party from displaying or distributing printed advertisements, handbills, etc., or from incurring election expenses for the purpose of promoting or opposing a candidate or party during an election campaign. The law did not preclude expenditures outside an election period, or even during an election period by a special interest group promoting or opposing a cause, as long as the group did not promote or oppose an election candidate. The purpose of the law was to protect the integrity of the spending limits on parties and candidates, because if third-party spending was unlimited, then a candidate with wealthy friends or the support of a wealthy special-interest group would have a distinct advantage over another candidate in the election campaign.

However, soon afterward, a court challenge was brought against the law, which resulted in it being struck down under the guarantee of freedom of expression in Canada's Charter of Rights and Freedoms. The court decision came just before the 1984 federal election; as a result the law was not enforced during that election, and the newly-elected federal Conservative government decided not to appeal the decision to a higher court. Third-party advertising was minimal during the 1984 election, but during the 1988 election the level of third-party activity increased dramatically. The Free Trade Agreement was a central issue in the election, and the political parties were identified closely with either side of the issue. Corporations and individuals spent huge amounts of money supporting their side of the campaign, and the issue arose again as to how limits could be put on third-party spending.

Though Canada's election financing system has many

admirable aspects, the third-party spending issue and other problems remain. The Chief Electoral Officer of Canada made extensive recommendations for improvements, and in 1991 the federal government's Royal Commission on Electoral Reform and Party Financing examined and proposed solutions to many of the issues in its reports.

A REAS OF LEADERSHIP IN AID TO DEVELOPING COUNTRIES

Canada's program of aid to developing countries is multi-faceted and involves people, organizations, ideas and technology. The Canadian International Development Agency (CIDA) administers the program and Canada's contribution to international development in the form of bilateral assistance, matching grants to nongovernmental organizations to help expand the scope and effect of their work, and other forms of financial and cooperative assistance. In 1989, CIDA spent about $2.7 billion on foreign aid projects. There are numerous organizations involved in the program.

The International Development Research Centre's (IDRC's) contribution to the development of technology in the third world has not only been unique, none of the countries which have tried to institute similar programs has been able to duplicate it. Created as an autonomous public corporation in 1970 by an Act of Parliament, IDRC funds scientific and technological research by indigenous scientists in developing countries. Over $105 million of government funding is spent annually. A nongovernmental, international board of twenty-one people, ten of whom are not Canadian and six of whom are from the developing world, decides which projects are to be funded. The decisions and policies are not connected with the Canadian government and, with some exceptions, are not required to have any Canadian content. This policy is unique in the world for a federally-funded organization. Such freedom allows IDRC to be responsive and "link people and plant seeds across national boundaries." All research projects are required to be practical, serve the needs of the region or country, and have the widest helpful effect possible.

CUSO (formerly Canadian University Students Overseas), SUCO (formerly Service Universitaire Canadien Outre-mer), Canada

World Youth, Canadian Crossroads International, World University Service of Canada (WUSC) all recruit and send students and skilled individuals to developing countries for cross-cultural exchanges and to help train people in various areas. CUSO was formed by representatives of twenty-one universities and twenty-two organizations from across Canada and overseas on September 22, 1961, three months after the U.S. Peace Corps. Since then, CUSO has sent about eight thousand volunteers of all ages to fill temporary staffing requirements in developing countries on two-year contracts. Canada World Youth and Canadian Crossroads International send mainly students on four- to six-month educational and cultural tours. WUSC sends students for six-week terms to another country to complete a research project on some facet of the country's development.

Canadian Executive Service Overseas (CESO), is a private, nonprofit Canadian corporation organized in 1967 by a group of Canadian business people with the cooperation of CUSO and the encouragement of the federal External Aid Office. CESO conducts exchanges with developing countries of applied professional and technical knowledge using experienced Canadians in the operation of projects in these countries. It also operates joint ventures with developing countries and a consultation program to assist native Canadian Indian peoples in establishing businesses.

Canada's programs also contribute to the education and improvement of Canada, through exposing students to different perspectives in the world, connecting Canadian business with international business ventures, and opening Canada up to technological innovations developed in other countries under the IDRC programs. Unfortunately, CIDA's programs, like those in other industrialized countries, have often benefitted Canada to the detriment of the people in the developing countries. Critics cite problems such as lack of accountability in decision-making, lack of citizen access to the planning process for many projects, the continuing requirement in some projects that aid be tied to purchases of Canadian goods and services, failures to monitor aid programs to ensure proper spending of funds and transfers of knowledge and expertise, and CIDA's lack of concern regarding the social and environmental damage caused by some of its projects. Recent examples of CIDA's problems in these areas include: its financial assistance in the environmental assessment of the Three Gorges dam in the Yangtze River in China (which would displace one million people and speed up soil erosion and desertification); its financing of a $4.7 million food irradiation project in Thailand (and another in Jamaica); its $2.2 million payment for 72 miles (116 kilometers) of steel rails not needed for an Indonesian railway project; and its $1.7 million in aid to Ethiopia to help with the resettlement of 1.5 million Ethiopians from the highlands to the lowlands (a move which led to the cutting of Ethiopia's remaining forests). So while there are some Canadian firsts in the area of making links with developing countries, many steps remain to be taken to separate aid (helping others) from trade (helping Canadians).

F IRST OMBUDSMAN IN NORTH AMERICA

"Ombudsman" is the Swedish word for "agent" or "representative". The ombudsman's role is to investigate complaints made by private citizens about injustice or abuse on the part of the government or the public service. Of course, as soon as an ombudsman is appointed, it would seem that the citizens have yet another public official; but the system appears to be working, as evidenced by the number of Canadian provinces that have taken up the practice.

The office originated in Sweden in 1809 and has also been used in New Zealand. Canada first took it up on April 6, 1967, when George Brinton McClellan (b.1908) was named ombudsman of Alberta. McClellan was a former Commissioner of the Royal Canadian Mounted Police (R.C.M.P.) and the first ombudsman in Canada and North America. Though there is still no federal ombudsman in Canada, many provincial legislatures have them. New Brunswick followed Alberta's lead and appointed its first ombudsman in October 1967. In 1969, Quebec appointed its first ombudsman (called Protecteur du citoyen), then Manitoba in 1970; Nova Scotia followed in 1971; Saskatchewan in 1973; Newfoundland and Ontario did the same in 1975 and then finally British Columbia in 1979. Only Prince Edward Island is without an ombudsman.

PUBLIC LENDING RIGHT COMMISSION (PLRC)

The Canadian government has recently shown itself to be firm in its commitment to authors and to the art of writing. People in Canada realize that "it is virtually impossible to survive by the pen alone" there because of the small population, whereas in the United States it is possible for authors to survive without subsidies because the book-buying market is that much larger. After fifteen years of hesitation and debate, and forty-seven years after the idea was first conceived, the federal government finally established a three-million-dollar annual fund in January, 1986, to compensate authors, editors, translators, and illustrators for the use of their books in libraries. The program was set up by the Minister of Communications in April,1986, to be administered by the Public Lending Right Commission (PLRC) of the Canada Council. The PLRC is composed of two commissions, one of twenty-four people who meet twice each year and handle major decisions, and an Executive Commission of seven people who meet six times a year to administer the fund. Canada is the thirteenth country to establish such a program; others include Sweden, which originated the program in the 1940s, England, Germany, Australia and Belgium.

Originally, the money allocated to authors was to be in proportion to the frequency at which their books are checked out of libraries. This turned out to be impossible to catalog and with the number of writers registered with the program, totalling about eight thousand as of April 1990, the fund would have been spread so thin as to be a negligible contribution to the authors' income. So the PLRC undertook a study and in October 1986 came up with fifteen representative libraries (ten English and five French) in terms of quality, quantity and geographical area. Authors are paid for the public use of their work(s) according to the number of libraries in which their work(s) are found out of the fifteen representative libraries. The maximum payment per work, if an author's work is found in ten libraries, is four hundred dollars (forty dollars per library), and the maximum that can be paid to any author is four thousand dollars. In 1990, about one hundred twenty authors earned the maximum amount. The amounts awarded are less for editors and translators. The PLRC sent out the first round of payments on April 17, 1987, and in 1990 dispensed $5.2 million to about sixty-five hundred authors.

Opponents of the system included librarians, who felt that the payment for the public lending right was an insult to the principle behind libraries, that people have the right to inform themselves free of charge. This tradition dates back to 1606 in Canada, when Marc Lescarbot founded the first public library in the Western Hemisphere at Port Royal, Nova Scotia. Librarians were also concerned about being compensated for the time they put into providing information to the program. They have been paid for their time and the manual searches to catalog the existence of a book in a library were done by students to save costs. Now being fine-tuned for the next round of payments, the Commission is exploring the idea of lifting the ceiling on the amount that one author can receive—a move which would cost an estimated three hundred thousand dollars per year—and the idea of refining the eligibility requirement to make the program more universal. Currently, directories, atlases, how-to books, textbooks, self-help books, catalogs and other works are excluded from the program.

The program is meant to afford Canadian writers more time to practice their art, and encourage the continued development of Canadian writing, libraries and authors. There have been efforts in the United States to set up a similar program.

D RUG PATENT LEGISLATION— Foremost until 1987

Investigations of the pharmaceutical industry in Canada in the 1960s by the Restrictive Trade Practices Commission (1963), the Hall Royal Commission on Health Services (1964) and the Harley Special Committee of the House of Commons on Drug Costs and Prices (1967) all found that drug prices in Canada were too high and recommended government action to stimulate price competition in the industry. The recommendations differed in nature but all were intended to deal with the seventeen-year patent periods for newly developed drugs granted to the mainly foreign-based multinational drug companies that dominated the Canadian drug industry. The extended period was seen as the root cause for the unduly high drug prices.

In 1969, these recommendations became Section 41(4) of the amended Patent Act. Section 41(4) allowed companies that wished to import and sell generic equivalents of patented brand-name drugs to do so upon receipt of a "compulsory licence" and upon payment of a 4 percent royalty to the company holding the patent for the particular drug. It created Canada's unique compulsory licensing system, a compromise between the complete abolition of drug patents or the stimulation of price competition while maintaining the principle of patent protection.

The system proved its worth in the following years, a conclusion reached by a comprehensive report released in May 1985 by the federal government's Commission of Inquiry on the Pharmaceutical Industry. The Commission, headed by Professor Harry Eastman of the University of Toronto, estimated that the price competition stimulated by compulsory licensing saved consumers at least $211 million in 1983. Savings for 1986 were projected to be $350 million.

In practice, it usually took four years for generic competitors to gain administrative and regulatory clearance to market generic copies of drugs. The Commission also found that "compulsory licensing has not had a discernible negative impact on the profitability and rate growth of the pharmaceutical industry as a whole." Total employment in the industry in Canada rose between 1967 and 1982 at a faster rate than in the U.S. and was not dominated by growth in the generic sector.

The Canadian government under Prime Minister Brian Mulroney, elected in September 1984, decided to dismantle the compulsory licensing system. Large multinational drug companies, many of them from the U.S., had argued for years that the Canadian system was unfair, and that it had a negative impact on investment in new drug research. They maintained that patents and higher prices were necessary to recover company investment in both successful and unsuccessful new drugs. On June 27, 1986, the Mulroney government succumbed to this pressure and to pressure from the Reagan administration, introducing Bill C-22, which proposed a ten-year period of patent protection for new drugs, and the creation of a Drug Price Review Board, charged with controlling price increases. Relying on promises from drug manufacturers to increase research investment in Canada and to limit price increases to the rate of inflation and increases in the consumer price index, the government began its push to turn the bill into law.

They were confronted with opposition from many groups.

The opposition parties in the House of Commons forced fourteen votes, delaying the bill's second reading in Parliament. Ninety-eight witnesses representing forty-six different groups gave testimony in twenty-four sessions of hearings before the standing committee responsible for the bill. The opposition parties introduced forty-seven amendments to the bill when it was debated again in Parliament, and after five more days of procedural maneuvers, the government was finally able to invoke closure on the debate over the bill.

But the opposition didn't end there. The Consumers Association of Canada (CAC), the Canadian Labour Congress, the National Action Committee on the Status of Women, the Canadian Council on Social Development, the National Anti-Poverty Organization, the National Pensioners and Senior Citizens Federation, and the Canadian Federation of University Women all opposed the bill. Polls showed that two-thirds of Canadians opposed the bill. Studies showed that the amount of research and development made by the pharmaceutical manufacturers had remained constant at about 4 percent of profits between 1967 and 1982, before and after compulsory licensing. Their promise to spend $1.4 billion more on research and development than they "would have" invested and create three thousand jobs in Canada by 1995 was seen as being a very unlikely positive effect of the bill. And the promise of price controls was seen to be equally tenuous. The Drug Price Review Board's monumental task was revealed to be the monitoring of thirty-five hundred drugs on the market with an annual budget of six hundred thousand dollars and a staff of six.

Andrew Cohen of the CAC summed up the opposition to the bill best when he said, "The purchase of drugs is not discretionary. If the drugs get too expensive you can't just buy apples instead. So we want controls on what happens in that marketplace. The drug companies and the government think there are investments and jobs to be won by safeguarding patents. But there's a price to be paid for those gains; the government thinks the price is worth it and we don't. It's as simple as that."

The Canadian Senate didn't think it was worth it either. In August 1987, the Senate rejected the House of Commons' version of the bill by a vote of forty to zero, and sent back their own amended version back to the House. Their amendments followed the Eastman Commission's recommendations of a four-year patent protection period, continued compulsory licensing, and higher royalties

(14 percent) to companies that actually do research in Canada. This move by the Liberal-dominated, appointed Senate was seen as a direct constitutional challenge to the will of the elected Conservative majority in the House of Commons. In response, the House voted to send the original version of the bill back to the Senate, and the Senate stalled passage of the bill once again.

Then, on October 9, the *Globe and Mail* revealed that the Mulroney government, in contrast to its repeated claims, had agreed to pass Bill C-22 as part of the free-trade agreement with the U.S. The Canadian government made the pledge in writing on October 3 in a signed but unreleased version of the deal, but the statement was left out of the subsequent version of the agreement, made public on October 4. This renewed the Senate's concern about other guarantees the government had made about the bill, and three weeks later they voted to send a version of the bill back to the House with the research and development and price control promises written into the legislation.

Once again, the House rejected the Senate's version of the bill and this time, on November 19, the Senate "stepped back from the brink of constitutional crisis" and allowed the House version to become law. The Conservative minority in the Senate passed the bill by a vote of twenty-seven to three; three Liberal Senators voted against the bill and thirty-two abstained.

With the vote, Canada's unique compulsory licensing system for pharmaceuticals, a system that was among the best in the world in terms of controlling drug prices while compensating originators of new drugs, was dismantled in favor of the U.S. system of no price controls, and an extensive patent protection system. A Canadian first and foremost was lost in the process.

CANADA'S ANTI-SMOKING CAMPAIGN

Canada leads the countries of the world in 1992 with its push to kick the tobacco habit. First of all, Air Canada became the only major airline in North America to offer smokeless flights when it began its program in April 1986 on flights between three Canadian cities. Encouraged by a favorable response from passengers and in terms of additional revenue, Air Canada extended the ban on April

26, 1987, to include flights between Toronto and New York.

Canada's federal government has initiated a national anti-smoking campaign. The goal is to produce a "new generation of non-smokers" by the year 2000. Aimed at young Canadians, the campaign includes a smoking-prevention program for pre-adolescents, an eight-part public relations kit to guide local and provincial prevention efforts, and a newsletter highlighting anti-smoking initiatives by governments and health organizations. In accordance with government regulations, federal government offices restricted smoking to specially designated areas on October 1, 1987, and as of January 1, 1989, smoking was banned in all federal workplaces. Canada also held the world's first tobacco-free Olympic Games at Calgary in February 1988, involving a smoking ban in the athletes' village, at all events, and on vehicles travelling to and from the Olympic site.

Even more extensive government measures include a $33.5 million tobacco diversification program, which involves compensation for tobacco growers who leave the industry, and a controversial law passed by Parliament that bans or restricts all tobacco advertising, promotion and brand sponsorship in Canada. Canada's Health and Welfare Minister at the time, Jake Epp, introduced the legislation, Bill C-51, (the Tobacco Products Control Act) on April 30, 1987. In presenting the legislation, he said "Cigarette smoking is the leading preventable health problem in our country. I believe that this new legislation will help to ensure that tobacco advertising no longer misrepresents the smoking habit as accompanying a glamorous lifestyle." Tobacco advertising has been banned in Norway, Finland and Singapore, leading to a decline in tobacco sales in Norway and a halt in the rise in sales in Finland.

The bill caught the tobacco manufacturers by surprise, triggering a multi-million dollar lobbying campaign by them in response. In July, 1987, tobacco manufacturers spent close to $576,000 on full-page newspaper advertisements across Canada explaining the issue to the public. They also mailed out packages of information on the issue to hundreds of thousands of Canadians, including pre-typed, pre-stamped letters opposing the legislation to be simply signed and sent to Members of Parliament. Despite their efforts, the bill passed by the majority Conservative government in the House of Commons on June 28, 1988, and came into effect January 1, 1989.

The law banned newspaper and magazine advertising

immediately, although magazines and newspapers imported from the United States containing cigarette advertising were not banned. TV and radio advertising was also banned, but companies had voluntarily withdrawn this form of advertising in 1972. Billboards and transit posters were required to have a new health warning 20 percent the size of the sign by July 1, 1989; they were banned as of January 1, 1991. Point of sale ads will be banned as of January 1, 1993. All forms of corporate sponsorship were restricted to the same level of funding that existed prior to January 1, 1988, and events are not allowed to show any depictions of cigarettes or the emblems used on cigarette packages. In response, many tobacco companies have set up new corporations with the cigarette brand name as the corporate name and with similar emblems as the corporate logo, and have used these corporations to sponsor events. Canada's three largest manufacturers of cigarettes, Imperial Tobacco Ltd. of Montreal, Rothmans Benson & Hedges Inc. and RJR-Macdonald, both of Toronto, also launched separate lawsuits in January 1989, arguing that the ban on advertising is unconstitutional because it infringes on their right to freedom of expression which is protected under the Canadian Charter of Rights and Freedoms. The Quebec Superior Court decided in July 1991, in one of the cases, that the legislation was unconstitutional but the government appealed. The decision from the Quebec Court of Appeal is expected by the end of 1992. The other cases have been put on hold until this case proceeds through the Canadian courts.

In 1989, Perrin Beatty replaced Jake Epp as Canada's Health and Welfare Minister. In January 1990, Beatty hinted in a speech that he would be introducing further regulations on cigarette packages and advertising. A proposal outlining the regulations was published on March 1, 1990. The proposed regulations require that each cigarette package have health warnings in black and white that takes up 25 percent of the front and back of the package. Cartons of cigarettes are required to have health warnings printed on all sides so that they cannot be stacked in a way that hides the warnings. Finally, Canada became the first country to propose requiring that an insert be placed into each cigarette package giving further information on the adverse health effects of smoking. However, since Benoit Bouchard became Health and Welfare Minister, the proposed regulations have not come any closer to being enacted. In July 1992, Australia enacted regulations similar to Canada's proposals, which will be effective July 1, 1993.

In the spring of 1992, Canada introduced with the annual government budget an export tax on cigarettes and roll-your-own tobacco to prevent cross-border shopping and smuggling of Canadian brand name tobacco products from the U.S. into Canada. Once again, the tobacco companies launched a massive lobbying effort and eight weeks later the tax was withdrawn. The issue remains important, however, because through tax increases on tobacco products, Canada has reduced consumption of tobacco more than any other industrialized country, reducing teenage smoking by two-thirds since 1980.

The U.S. has the lowest taxes on tobacco products of any industrialized country. If the U.S. increased taxes on tobacco products to the level of other industrialized countries such as Canada, which now collects an average of $US3.26 per packet, teenage smoking would drop by two-thirds or more and adult smoking would fall substantially. Higher tobacco taxes would save more than 5 million lives over time, and would raise state and federal tobacco tax revenues to more than $40 billion from the 1991 level of $11 billion.

Food

McINTOSH APPLE

The most important fruit grown in Canada, in terms of dollar crop value, is the apple. Of all the types of Canadian apples, the most distinctive is the McIntosh red. The McIntosh resembles the first apples brought from Normandy to Port Royal, Nova Scotia, in 1606, which marked the beginning of the cultivation of the apple in Canada. This delicious fruit, well known all over North America, was discovered in 1811 by a new Canadian settler, John McIntosh (1777-1846), at Dundela, in Dundas County, Ontario.

McIntosh found a wild apple tree among the remnants of an abandoned farmhouse near his home, and since apples were hard to come by, he transplanted the tree onto his own land. When the apples ripened, he found that they were the best he had ever tasted, and his neighbors agreed. However, the seeds of apples do not produce exactly the same variety of tree, so he could not produce any more apples than the one tree would bear.

Finally, a hired hand who knew the art of grafting solved the problem, and John's son Alan set up a business travelling around the area selling branches of the tree. In 1906, the original tree on McIntosh's farm stopped bearing fruit. Still today, every McIntosh tree in the world and every McIntosh apple eaten are descendants of that original tree.

WHEAT

In 1754, the first wheat grown in the west was planted by Louis La Corne (1703-61), on the south shore of the North Saskatchewan River in central Saskatchewan. But full scale agricultural development of the Canadian west was inhibited by its short growing season. The introduction of Red Fife wheat, discovered by David Fife of Ontario, into Manitoba in about 1875 was a major advance. Western farmers grew it widely and successfully for the next forty years, but it too was often damaged by early frosts. The development of Marquis wheat by Canadian Sir Charles Saunders (1867-1937) was what the farmers in the west had been waiting for. This strain of wheat, which took as little as one hundred days to ripen, was first distributed to farmers in 1909; by 1920, 90 percent of the wheat planted in western Canada was of the Marquis strain. There was also a large acreage in the United States. In terms of financial return to the Canadian economy, Saunder's development ranks among the outstanding contributions of science and technology. When he died, the *Daily Express* of London wrote that "he contributed more to the wealth of his country than any other man."

Originally, Saunders was trained as a musician at the University of Toronto and Johns Hopkins University and did not have any desire to work on plant breeding experiments. He devoted the years between 1894 and 1903 to teaching music and voice. But in 1903, Saunders was in his mid-thirties, married, and unable to find a suitable job in his chosen profession. He finally accepted the job his strong-willed father had created for him as an experimentalist in the Experimental Farms Service at Dominion Cerealist in Ottawa. Charles inherited the previous decade of experiments that had been completed by his father, who was head of the Canadian Horticultural Society.

Marquis wheat developed out of a cross between Red Fife, a rust-resistant, fast-maturing Canadian variety, and an Indian wheat called Hard Red Calcutta, that had been accomplished by Percy Saunders in 1892. The resulting strain had been labelled "Markham Wheat." It did not produce uniform offspring so Saunders carefully selected individual heads from early plants and emphasized that seed from each plant without mixing strains. The best strain to come out of his experiments matured one week before Red Fife, produced high yields and excellent bread. Saunders named it "Marquis Wheat." The rest, as they say, is history.

Subsequently, Saunders was instrumental in developing Ruby, Garnet and Reward wheats, all adapted especially to prairie conditions. He was knighted in 1934 for his contribution. The government rewarded Saunders with a pension of nine hundred dollars a year for his efforts, but under pressure from grateful wheat farmers whose lives had been changed by Marquis wheat, the government increased Saunders' pension to five thousand dollars a year in 1925.

Improvements to the combine

In 1938, another development occurred in Canada that would revolutionize wheat farming. Thomas Carroll, an Australian working at the Massey-Harris factory in Toronto, developed significant improvements to the combine, which, as its name suggests, combines the harvesting tasks of cutting, threshing, cleaning and delivering the grain into operation. The combine became known worldwide as the "Miracle of the Harvest." The Massey company, begun in 1847 by Daniel Massey near Cobourg, Ontario, would become Massey-Ferguson, one of Canada's best known establishments and a world leader in the manufacturing of farm machinery.

PABLUM

Pablum. Is it intellectual sustenance or tasteless writing? Actually, it's a Canadian-born baby food. Three concerned physicians at the Hospital for Sick Children (HSC) in Toronto were responsible for the breakfast cereal that has become a household word to parents with infants. This first pre-cooked, vitamin-enriched cereal was invented in the late 1920s by Doctors T.G.H. Drake, Alan Brown, and Frederick F. Tisdall. The name is derived from the Greek *pabulum* for food.

At first the doctors devised a vitamin biscuit, but then they came up with the idea of a pre-cooked cereal. The ingredients sound like the stock on the shelves of one of today's health-food stores: wheat meal, oatmeal, cornmeal, wheat germ, bone meal, dried brewer's yeast, and alfalfa. With this cereal, every child could get an instant, nutritional breakfast that was easy for parents to prepare.

Pablum was first marketed internationally by Mead Johnson in 1930. Since then its sales have generated substantial income for the HSC in the form of royalties donated to the Hospital's Pediatric Research Foundation (See Hospital for Sick Children). In

1991, Pablum fed about 110,000 babies in Canada. Today, Pablum is manufactured and sold solely in Canada.

F ROZEN FOOD

Dr. Archibald G. Huntsman (1883-1973) was a marine scientist on the Biological Board of Canada (later the Fisheries Research Board) in Halifax in 1926 when the Board decided to test the commercial possibilities of marketing high quality frozen fish. Within two years Huntsman had developed "Ice Fillets", which the Board introduced in the Toronto market in 1929, the first time packaged, quick-frozen food was offered for sale to the public. The product was immediately popular despite its relatively high price. During 1929 alone the Board, along with two private companies, Lunenberg Sea Products Co, and the Lockeport Co., sold more than 50 metric tons of Ice Fillets, mostly in the Toronto area, but also in Halifax, Montreal, Ottawa, and as far west as Winnipeg, Manitoba.

Notwithstanding the initial success of the demonstration, however, the fishing industry and trade soon lost interest in the innovation, and in 1931 the experiment was terminated. Huntsman was somewhat bitter: "We did it," he commented, "we showed them how, and in the opinion of the industry on the Atlantic coast, the continuation of what we started in Toronto was killed deliberately by the wholesale fish dealer who distributed the fish. He was against it, although he handled it, because it was in competition with the stale fish that he sold otherwise."

Whatever the reason for it—the Board, to be fair, had never intended to go into full-scale commercial production, and the two private companies that had shown interest did not have and could not find the financial resources needed to allow them to do so—the decision to terminate opened the way for an American, Colonel Clarence Birdseye, to claim credit for inaugurating the frozen foods industry. Birdseye had been working on the concept independently since 1917, and from 1924 his Gloucester, Massachusetts-based company, General Seafoods, had been trying to develop a commercially viable process. It was not until after he sold out to the Postum Company that his work got the kind of financial backing it needed to achieve commercial success. The first "Birds Eye" frozen foods were put on the market on March 6, 1930.

INSTANT FOODS

In 1960, Dr. Edward Asselbergs, head of food processing at the Food Research Institute in Ottawa, set out to develop instant meat, fish, chicken and cheese products. The intent was to produce dried products for export to northern Europe where there was a shortage of high-protein food and inadequate refrigeration.

By 1962, Asselbergs' group had produced instant foods in powdered form that were less bulky and less susceptible to spoilage than fresh, frozen or cured foods. The researchers found that instant mashed potato was the key ingredient in a recipe for the range of protein-rich instant foods. If the potato was added to ground meat or cheese before drying, it effectively separated the meat and cheese so they did not lump together into rubbery granules or a hard, fibrous mass.

By the time Asselberg and his researchers had completed their work, they found that conditions in northern Europe had improved considerably and that others seemed to be the most likely beneficiaries. Whether exported to protein-hungry developing countries, prepared as food for campers or in military field rations, bought by people who want instant foods high in protein, or as an alternative to snack foods lacking in nutrition, Asselbergs' instant foods have found a place in the eating habits of the world today.

CHOCOLATE BAR

Necessity is not the only mother of invention; sometimes it's a fishing trip. In 1872, James H. Ganong (1841-88) founded a small bakery and candy shop in St. Stephen, New Brunswick, where the St. Croix River flows into Passamaquoddy Bay. The family business, called Ganong Brothers Limited, expanded rapidly as a chocolate manufacturer. In 1910, Arthur D. Ganong and factory supervisor George F. Ensor invented and introduced the five-cent chocolate nut bar. Fishing was their excuse; many of their customers made their living (or found their recreation) on the water, and the chocolate bar was convenient for taking along on fishing trips. Still located in St. Stephen, but in a new facility, the company continues to be successful, with David A. Ganong as president and R.W. Ganong as chair of the only family-owned, large confectionary company in Canada.

G INGER ALE

Most people consider Canada Dry virtually synonymous with ginger ale, but only about three people in the world today know the patented formula for the ginger ale and the company is not in the business of publicizing their names. In 1890, John J. McLaughlin, a graduate of the University of Toronto and a chemist and pharmacist, founded a soda water bottling plant in Toronto. McLaughlin had earned a Gold Medal in pharmacy while at the University, but it was his business sense that helped him revolutionize an industry. In 1904, he began to develop his own flavoring extracts for the soda water sold then. He also developed techniques for mass bottling, making his "soft drinks" available outside of the soda fountains and drugstores.

McLaughlin marketed what he called "McLaughlin Belfast Style Ginger Ale", the first version of his ginger ale. In 1904, his company introduced "Pale Dry Ginger Ale", the early forebear of Canada Dry ginger ale with a label depicting a beaver sitting on top of a map of Canada. In 1907, he patented his creation as "Canada Dry Ginger Ale" and his company, Canada Dry Ltd., grew rapidly, bottling "the champagne of ginger ales" at a Sherbourne Street plant in Toronto. That year Canada Dry products were accepted by appointment to the Royal Household of the governor general of Canada. The beaver on the label was replaced by the crown and shield, but the now famous map of Canada remained.

McLaughlin died in 1914 and the business was taken over by his brothers, who considered expanding the thriving business beyond Canada's borders. In 1921, the ginger ale was introduced into the United States and a U.S. subsidiary was opened in New York City, with P.D. Saylor as general manager of that plant. It was an overnight success in America and in 1931 a U.S. subsidiary bought the original Canadian company. It has changed hands several times since then. Currently, Canada Dry Limited, a strictly Canadian operation now under the name Cadbury Beverages Canada Incorporated, is owned by the U.S. subsidiary of the British Cadbury-Schweppes Corporation. Canada Dry products became popular in the United States and are now sold throughout in ninety countries on six continents.

Environment

FIRST BIRD SANCTUARY IN NORTH AMERICA

In the early 1900s American-born Jack Miner, a naturalist, writer, and lecturer on conservation, founded what is now a world famous bird sanctuary at his farm at Kingsville, Ontario. The sanctuary was the first of its kind in North America. Miner (1865-1944) began his study of migratory bird habits at the sanctuary in 1909. He banded a Mallard duck in August of that year, scratching his address on a small piece of aluminum which he attached to the duck and then released. The duck was shot on January 14, 1910, at Anderson, South Carolina, and the tag returned to Miner by the hunter, completing the first banding record in North America. Miner's study greatly influenced conservation laws in North America, and he initiated a tagging system that helped prove that birds migrate great distances. Miner banded over fifty thousand birds himself between 1910 and 1915. Before Miner's work, naturalists had only guessed at the migratory habits of birds.

In 1943, Miner was rewarded for his efforts when he received the Order of the British Empire "for the greatest achievement in Conservation in the British Empire." After Miner's death, the Canadian government declared the week of his birthday (April 10) as National Wildlife Week to honor the work he accomplished in the preservation of bird life.

Another conservation park in Canada, Provincial Wildlife Park in Shubenacadie, Nova Scotia, is known internationally for its breeding of rare waterfowl. It was the first park to breed in captivity the Atlantic brant and ring-necked and American eider ducks. Since 1980, the park has been one of several parks successfully breeding endangered Hawaiian geese. Only thirty-three of the geese were alive in 1954 but the population is now estimated at three thousand to thirty-five hundred.

SLICKLICKER

On February 4, 1970, the Liberian-registered tanker *Arrow* ran aground, spilling ten thousand metric tons of oil onto the water and beaches of Chedabucto Bay, Nova Scotia. Then four "Slicklickers" went to work, lifting two hundred thousand gallons of oil off the surface of rough seas in ten weeks. Invented by Richard Sewell in the late 1960s while he was working as a chemist for the Defence Research Board of the Department of National Defence in Canada, the Slicklicker is a simple machine that can lift as much as forty-three thousand gallons of oil off the water in twenty-four hours. According to Dr. McTaggart-Cowan, head of the Canadian task force that cleaned up the Chedabucto Bay spill, the Slicklicker is "the best machine for oil clean-up in the world, I should know, I tried them all."

Inventor Sewell's brilliant machine is based on the fact that oil attracts oil and repels water. Surface oil near the Slicklicker is trapped by an inflatable plastic boom with a five-foot skirt mounted on a barge or boat. A three-foot-wide oil-soaked conveyor belt made of canvas and terry cloth is circulated through the boom, soaking up oil and then wringing it out into drums.

The Slicklicker has many advantages over older methods of cleaning up spills. It salvages most of the oil for reuse, it is relatively cheap and compact, it doesn't harm the environment, and it is portable and and works well in rough seas. In the early 1970s Richard Sewell and his brother George founded RBH Cybernetics Patents and Processes, Ltd., to manufacture Slicklickers. Approximately forty-five Slicklickers had been sold by mid-1972. To date, fifty Slicklickers are in use around the world. Thirty have been sold to the Canadian government for use in harbors, ten to the U.S. Navy, and others to the governments of England, Japan, France, Israel and Okinawa. The last one was sold to Borneo in 1981, the year the Sewell brothers, facing rising production costs and overwhelming competition from companies manufacturing a similar product, halted production of the Slicklicker.

GREENPEACE

In 1970, the ad hoc Don't Make a Wave Committee was formed in Vancouver to protest U.S. nuclear tests at Amchitka in the middle of the Aleutian National Wildlife Reserve. The following year, the Greenpeace Foundation was formed out of this committee by Jim Bohlen, an engineer by training; lawyer Irving Stone; and law student Paul Cote. After emigrating from California where he had worked with the Sierra Club for fifteen years, Bohlen had set up and was chairperson of the Canadian Sierra Club. When the Club didn't want to get involved with the Amchitka testing, Bohlen decided to form the new group. In their first direct action, eleven members of the group set sail in a chartered trawler boat, christened *Greenpeace*, into the bomb testing range and got enough attention to upset Canadians living downwind of the test site and to bring the matter before the U.S. Supreme Court. The U.S. bomb testing only added to the anger people felt over the radiation that had been carried over eastern Canada from Nevada nuclear test sites. Greenpeace was successful and the four additional tests at Amchitka were cancelled.

Greenpeace has had many firsts in protesting violations of our environment. In 1972 and 1973, Greenpeace mounted expeditions to Mururoa Island in protest of the French government's testing of nuclear weapons in the South Pacific. On July 15, 1973, the group's yacht, *Greenpeace III*, sailed into the security zone around the test site to protest the tests. The yacht was boarded and seized by French sailors, but the publicity created by the efforts of Greenpeace members forced the French to move the tests underground. On June 17, 1975, a French court ordered the French government to compensate Greenpeace member David McTaggart, who chose the name Greenpeace for the group, for the damage done to *Greenpeace III* when it was rammed and boarded by the French in 1972. On July 10, 1985, the Greenpeace flagship, the *Rainbow Warrior*, was in the harbor at Auckland, New Zealand, on its way to test the waters around Mururoa Island for radiation leaks from the underground nuclear tests, when it was bombed and sank, killing a photographer aboard the trawler. Two members of the French security service have been convicted of the bombing and imprisoned. As Jim Bohlen (former Executive Director of Greenpeace and now on the Board of Directors of Greenpeace Canada) states, such a reaction from a "responsible" government to Greenpeace is one measure of its effectiveness.

The effectiveness of Greenpeace can be seen in other reactions to the group's actions. Twenty campaigns against the whaling industry have produced a virtual ban on whaling. Only Iceland and Japan disregard the International Whaling Commission's ruling on whaling. On numerous occasions, Greenpeace has plugged discharge pipes of companies that are illegally dumping hazardous wastes. The publicity garnered usually enrages the public and forces regulatory agencies to take action. Bohlen claims, "No Greenpeacer has ever gone to jail. It would be politically incorrect. As individuals we are weak. Our strength is created by putting ourselves at risk."

Greenpeace is now one of the largest environmental groups in the world, with offices in Argentina, Australia, Austria, Belgium, Canada, Costa Rica, Denmark, Ireland, West Germany, Finland, France, Italy, Japan, Luxembourg, Netherlands, New Zealand, Norway, Spain, Sweden, Switzerland, United Kingdom, the United States, and the former U.S.S.R. Since 1988, Greenpeace headquarters have been located in Amsterdam, from where the group maintains its objective of "a moratorium on all those things poisoning us," according to Bohlen.

Science

NOBEL PRIZE RECIPIENTS IN SCIENCE ASSOCIATED WITH CANADA

Canadians are generally aware of at least one Canadian Nobel Prize recipient, namely Frederick G. Banting who shared the 1923 Nobel Prize for physiology or medicine with John J.R. MacLeod for the discovery of insulin (See Insulin in the section entitled Medicine). However, Canada has a number of other Nobel Prize's for scientific work associated with it either because the work was done in Canada, or the recipient was Canadian.

Ernest Rutherford—Foremost Model of the Atom

Almost every high school student who has taken chemistry or physics has heard of Ernest Rutherford's model of the atom. Rutherford (1871-1937), who formed the foundations for the atomic and nuclear physics, did most of his work at McGill University in Montreal. Born in Nelson, New Zealand, Rutherford went to England early in his career to work and study. Though he was very respected for his achievements there, he was not accepted for a fellowship at Trinity College at Cambridge, in part, he felt, because of the prevailing Cambridge snobbery towards those who had been undergraduates elsewhere, especially in the colonies. He entered a competition for a professorship at McGill University and became the MacDonald Professor of Physics there in 1898, in charge of the MacDonald

Physics Laboratory. He occupied the chair of experimental physics at McGill from 1898 to 1907.

His main contribution to science was his elaboration in 1902 on the disintegration theory of the atom, the structure of the atom and the principles of radioactivity, work that completely transformed the meaning of the discovery of radioactivity and recognized the enormous energy potential of atomic fission. In 1908, he won the Nobel Prize for chemistry for this theoretical work done at McGill, and he was later knighted for his contributions to science. He collaborated with many scientists, including the British chemist Frederick Soddy, (1877-1956), who worked at McGill from 1900 to 1902 and won the Nobel prize for chemistry for related work in 1921. His interests and pursuits were always diverse while he was at McGill, and he frequently had several projects underway at once. Encompassing the major fields of physics, radioactivity, atomic and nuclear physics in his work, Rutherford is thought to have contributed more than any other to the present views concerning the nature of matter.

Gerhard Herzberg

Born in Hamburg, Germany, in 1904, Herzberg began his scientific work early in his life and had already published twenty scientific papers by 1929, when he was twenty-four. The Nazi persecution of Jews forced Herzberg to emigrate to Canada in 1935, and soon afterward he became a research professor at the University of Saskatchewan. However, he was classified as an enemy alien and so played no role in military research projects during World War II.

In 1945, Herzberg became a Canadian citizen and accepted a position as professor at the Yerkes Observatory of the University of Chicago. He returned to Canada in 1948 as principal research officer in the Division of Physics at the National Research Council in Ottawa. The following year he was named director of the Division of Physics and in 1955 he became director of the Division of Pure Physics. In 1969, Herzberg was appointed distinguished research officer at the research council's Herzberg Institute of Astrophysics, the Council's highest grade created especially to allow Herzberg to continue his work after his official retirement that year.

Herzberg's work was mainly concerned with electromagnetic radiation, the energy in the form of a wave produced by electrical charges. He focused upon identifying the structure and energy levels of atoms and molecules using spectroscopic instruments (which analyze the line spectra of the light created when isolated atoms are exposed to electromagnetic radiation). Initially, Herzberg primarily studied the structure and properties of stable molecules. However, in the early 1950s he began analyzing so-called "free radicals", which are very reactive atoms and molecules that have very brief lifetimes and so had yet not been observed. Using newly developed techniques, Herzberg and his colleagues made the first successful spectroscopic studies of free methyl in 1956. Herzberg was awarded the 1971 Nobel Prize for chemistry for "his contributions to the knowledge of electronic structure and geometry of molecules, particularly free radicals."

Henry Taube

Born in Neudorf, Saskatchewan, in 1915, Henry Taube attended the University of Saskatchewan where he received a bachelor's degree in science in 1935 and a masters in science two years later. He then went to the University of California at Berkeley and has remained in the United States ever since. Taube became an American citizen in 1941 and since 1962 has been professor of chemistry at Stanford University and in 1978 was appointed as dean of the department.

Taube was awarded the 1983 Nobel Prize for chemistry for "his studies of the mechanisms of electron transfer reactions, particularly of metal complexes." This work mainly involved studying the bonding and reactions of metals in processes such as oxidation.

John C. Polyani

Born in Berlin, Germany, in 1929, John Polyani moved with his family to Manchester, England, when he was four years old. Polyani was raised and educated there and received his Ph.D. in chemistry from the University of Manchester in 1952. His studies at the university set the course for his future work on the molecular basis of chemical reactions. Specifically, Polyani searched for the answer to the question of what types of forces are most conducive to causing a chemical reaction when molecules collide.

Polyani did his post-doctoral work from 1952 to 1954 at

the laboratories of Canada's National Research Council (NRC) in Ottawa, and there he spent a few months in Gerhard Herzberg's laboratory measuring the motions of various molecular products. Polyani then spent two years in the United States as a post-doctoral fellow at Princeton University before returning to Canada in 1956 as a lecturer in chemistry at the University of Toronto. He was appointed professor of chemistry in 1962. His work from then on with many graduate students led to the measurement and confirmation in the late 1960s of the rates of various forces at which a chemical reaction would create molecular products with specific motions. This work and the work of others set the basis for the development of lasers. In 1986, Polyani shared the Nobel Prize for chemistry with Americans Dudley R. Herschbach and Yuan T. Lee for contributions to "the development of a new field of research in chemistry—reaction dynamics."

Polyani has also been active in public affairs since the late 1950s, particularly in relation to the problem of survival in an age of nuclear weapons. He became the founding chairperson of the Canadian Pugwash Group in 1960 and remained chairperson until 1978, and he is an active member of the Committee on International Security Studies of the U.S. National Academy of Sciences and of the Canadian Centre for Arms Control and Disarmament.

FIRSTS AND FOREMOSTS IN MAPS AND MAPPING

When faced with a great dilemma, a nation is often more inspired to find a solution. Such is the case with Canada and its geography and resources. Compared to the land mass it occupies, Canada's population has always been small. When the country was young, this huge land mass presented an abundance of resources. As it became apparent that Canada's economy would be based upon these resources, the necessity of figuring out their limitations and how they should be managed became an increasingly important problem. The development of mapping in Canada was a key step in solving this problem, and Canada has many achievements in the field that offer excellent examples of Canada's contribution to an international scientific field.

Second national atlas in the world

In 1906, the Department of the Interior of the Canadian government published *The Atlas of Canada*, its first national atlas and the second in the world after Finland's. The second enlarged edition was issued in 1915. A new atlas appeared in 1958, followed by a French version one year later. The fourth version, entitled *The National Atlas of Canada*, was published in 1973 (revised in 1976) and National Atlas Information, of the Surveys and Mapping Branch of the Energy, Mines and Resources Ministry, is currently producing the fifth enlarged, bilingual and multi-colored version of the atlas. It is being produced in a serial format: as each map is published it is made available for sale to the public through the Canada Map Office in Ottawa. The process began in 1983 and so far forty-five English and forty-five French maps have been published. The goal is to produce two hundred maps (not the complete series) by the end of the century.

First mapping camera calibrator

As the mapping needs of the world became more complex and aerial photographs began to be used, Canada's National Research Council (NRC) in Ottawa responded, leading the field. Today, 60 to 70 percent of mapping technology worldwide is based on Canadian developments. It all began with the development of the camera calibrator in 1945 by Dr. Les Howlett, then the Associate Director of Physics at the NRC. He eventually became director and is a member of the Royal Society of Canada. The calibrator set a standard for cameras used in aerial photography, and Canada was one of the first countries in the world to require these cameras to be calibrated once each year. Standard aerial photos were necessary in order to derive accurate maps from the photos.

First radar profile recorder

In 1947, the Division of Electrical Engineering at the NRC developed the radar profile recorder, a device that measured the time it took electronic pulses to travel from an airplane to the ground below and back. By correlating this figure with the altimeter readings of the plane, and aerial photos of the land, mappers were able to construct accurate three-dimensional models of the land, used to make topo-graphical maps.

First analytical plotter for mapping

In 1951, Polish-born Dr. T.J. Blachut, working in Switzerland at the time, was invited to head up the newly established Photogrammetic Research Section at the National Research Council. During and after World War II, mapping had been done using an analog plotter, so called because the plotter was used to create an analogous three-dimensional model of the land using physical means (such as two photographs taken from different points of reference to give a mapmaker three coordinates with which to construct a three-dimensional model for each point on the aerial photo).

In 1953, Dr. Blachut's division, led by Finnish-born U.V. Helava, began to develop a method to derive mathematically the coordinates needed to construct the three-dimensional models used in mapping. Called the Analytical Plotter, the device used a precise, stereoscopic (three-dimensional) viewing system and recorder hooked up to a computer and was able to simultaneously view an aerial photo and construct a three-dimensional model for a map of the area. The plotter can convert any photograph into a map because it uses geometrical and mathematical constructions, so any changes in scale, dimension or distortion in the photograph are simply factored into the construction of the three-dimensional model of the map.

The first version of the plotter was introduced in 1963 in Ottawa. A final, updated model was exhibited in Finland in 1976. According to Dr. Blachut, the development of the analytical plotter was revolutionary in the field and a greater achievement for mapping than the development of the jet airplane was for aviation. Unfortu-nately, as with many other brilliant Canadian inventions, no Canadian company would or could produce the plotter. Since there was not an industrial optics industry in Canada at the time, the NRC ended up selling the rights to the instrument to Nistri Company of Rome, Italy, which quickly received a trial order from the U.S. Air Force for twenty-five Analytical Plotters at a cost of $250,000 each. Once again, a Canadian inventor and leader in his field had looked behind him to see if he had followers and found none—only to see his ideas enthusiastically espoused elsewhere.

Development of the stereo-orthophotography mapping technique

In 1965, Dr, Blachut, along with Stanley Collins, developed the stereo-orthophotography technique, which allowed mapmakers to produce automatically aerial photos with the characteristics of a three-dimensional map. The device rectified the distortions varying terrain usually caused when aerial photos were converted into maps by automatically giving them the geometrical characteristics of a map. This provided a new type of mapping in the form of very precise scale aerial photographs with contours. By 1970, Blachut had developed an instrument, called a stereo compiler, that employed this technique. For those who needed traditional maps, Blachet also developed a technique for plotting maps from the stereo-ortho aerial photographs.

Development of the automatic image correlator and Gestalt Photo Mapper

Another development was made by G. Hobrough, while working at a small Toronto firm. Hobrough developed the world's first automatic image correlator, which was able to record depth as the human eye can by automatically recording contours and profiles of the area being viewed for the construction of three-dimensional models. Previously, mapping could be completed by taking the aerial photo and converting it into a map, but the correlator was able to "recognize" what was being recorded by the viewer and automatically convert into a precise shape on a three-dimensional model of the map. It completed this task about three hundred times faster than the analog plotter could.

In 1975, Hobrough and his company combined the analytical plotter and the automatic image correlator to produce automatically orthophotos and stereo-orthophotos, and a three-dimensional digital terrain model (recorded numerically on a computer). Mapping technique took a giant step forward. The instrument, called the Gestalt Photo Mapper (GPM), is the most advanced mapping technology in the world in the 1980s.

Photogrammetry techniques developed in Canada have also been used to screen thousands of school children for signs of scoliosis or curvature of the spine. After taking a contour photograph of the child's body illuminated from behind a screen, a nurse can make a quick diagnosis for scoliosis by looking for asymmetrical contours in the photograph. The National Research Council is also exploring other possible applications for the automatic image correlator, using it on the space shuttle to guide the Canadarm automatically in its operations, and as a guide for robotic manufacturing machines.

Today, the applications for Canada's mapping technology abound. Remarkably, about 60 to 70 percent of the world is still unmapped. This is especially true in developing countries, where it is crucial for them to know the extent and limitations of their natural resources so they can be developed properly and wisely. Decreases in available arable land, increases in the development of land and other key measurements in the monitoring of changes in the ambience of the surface of the earth can all be made using map analysis techniques called Geographic Information Systems.

Geographic Information Systems

Perhaps the most far reaching Canadian first related to mapping was the development of the first geographic information system. These are computer based systems that store many maps in digital form and allow them to be read, measured, and compared to produce useful information. If you have ever enjoyed looking at a map but were dismayed at the tedious business of measuring distances or calculating areas or of hand coloring special areas, then you can understand immediately why people are excited at seeing maps on a computer screen and by having the power of the computer available to read and analyze maps of all kinds. Now it is possible to have detailed electronic maps of an entire city, of the natural resources of an entire province or state, of environmentally sensitive areas of a continent or of country boundaries, roads, rivers, places and names of the whole globe on a desktop computer. Today, Geographic Information Systems (GIS) provide the potential for greater understanding of the complex relationships between humans and their environment in all levels of decision making: international, national, regional, municipal, local, and personal.

GIS originated in Canada in the early 1960s. Canada is a large country, and produces many maps but had a limited supply of trained persons to analyze the vast amount of information. It was the inspiration of Canadians to use early computers to analyze their maps. Early work by Dr. Roger Tomlinson led to a proposal in 1962, accepted by the Federal government, to fund feasibility studies in 1963, and to the development from 1964 to the present day of the Canada Geographic Information System (CGIS), the forerunner of today's systems. Dr. Tomlinson directed the development of CGIS from 1964 to 1969 and in the process named the field and laid the foundation for later developments worldwide.

Geographic information systems are now in use in thousands of locations in a myriad of applications from archaeology to zoology. They represent a fundamental new way of seeing and understanding the living space of humanity.

FIRST TO EXTRACT HELIUM FROM NATURAL GAS

In 1915, John Cunningham McLennan (1867-1935) of Ingersoll, Ontario, who spent his career as a professor of physics at the University of Toronto, designed equipment which could extract helium from natural gas being pumped in Calgary. McLennan graduated from the University in 1892 and then received his doctorate in physics there in 1900. He worked at the University from 1907 to 1932, making important contributions to research in low spectrometry, spectroscopy, radium treatment for cancer patients, and the magnetic detection of submarines. His discovery of the helium extraction process had the greatest effect. As a result, in 1918 the price of helium, which ranged from fifteen-hundred dollars to six thousand dollars per cubic foot, dropped to seventeen cents per cubic foot. McLennan was elected to the Royal Society of London that year and received its gold medal in 1928. He also served as the scientific adviser to the British Admiralty during World War I.

McLennan helped found the National Research Council while working in Canada and retired from the University of Toronto and moved to England in 1932, leaving behind the famous physics laboratory he built and which bears his name. On July 9, 1935, he was knighted for the scientific services he had provided.

FIRST WORKING ELECTRON MICROSCOPE IN NORTH AMERICA

It took an electron microscope six feet high to enable scientists to see and understand some of nature's most baffling, minute mysteries. Deadly bloodstream viruses, smoke particles, and the growth of crystals suddenly could be photographed and studied. During the period between 1935 and 1939, University of Toronto physics professor Eli Franklin Burton (1879-1948), working with his students Cecil Hall, James Hillier and Albert Prebus of Alberta, developed the first working model of an electron microscope in North America. Before their accomplishment, the most powerful microscope could only magnify an object a few hundred times its actual size. The electron microscope allowed researchers to magnify objects hundreds of thousands times their size.

Based on plans originally developed in Europe, the group developed and built a six-foot high microscope, equipped with a series of electrical coils that employed a stream of electrons, instead of a beam of light, to enlarge the object; the electrons were focused with magnetic fields instead of optical glass lenses, and the object was then reviewed when the electrons hit a fluorescent screen.

Burton was the son of a country grocer who ran a general store in the village of Green River, northeast of Toronto, where Burton was born. The family later moved to Toronto, and Burton's brother became one of the country's most successful and famous merchants, as president of the Robert Simpson Company. Eli turned his talent to science, and after his initial university work, and studies at Cambridge University, he returned to the University of Toronto. The Order of the British Empire was awarded to Burton for his work on radar equipment, one of Canada's most outstanding contributions to the war effort. Later in his life, he devoted himself to the role scientists could play in improving the welfare of humans; he concentrated on cancer research during this period. He remains most famous, however, for the development of his working model of the electron microscope.

CANADARM (Remote Manipulator System)—First of its kind

An arm, fifty feet long (fifteen meters), with muscles of electronic motors, nerves of copper wiring, bones of graphite fiber and reinforced tubing, skin a white insulated blanket with heaters attached to protect from the sun's intense heat and the frigid cold of the shadows, and controlled by a computer brain in space . . . Sound like science fiction? It's not! Something from outer space? Well, maybe. It's Canadarm, a marvel of Canadian imagination and ingenuity and now an essential tool for space development. Canadarm has become a familiar sight from news reports of the space shuttle.

The National Research Council of Canada scientists who developed Canadarm first faced the challenge to build Canadarm in 1975. Canada had already excelled at developing several types of extra-human extensions of the hand, including the hand-arm machine for industry and the electronic hand, but this extension of the ability of people to work in space presented a different challenge. There was no existing model or technology on which to base their assignment of making a machine that would work in the harsh atmosphere of space, with its extreme variations in temperature. In order to test the machine as it was being developed, scientists had to play a sort of Canadarm video game, for they couldn't test the arm in the weightless environment in which it would have to work. As it turns out, the arm can lift as much as 66,000 pounds (30,000 kilograms) in space, but on Earth it cannot lift its own weight off the ground.

In November 1981, on the second launch of the shuttle orbiter *Columbia*, the public first witnessed this amazing extension of human ability in space. Millions of people around the world watched as the mechanical arm reached into space, a small Canadian flag and the word "CANADA" proudly displayed on its side. Canadarm has a "hand", a wire snare device that fits over a special prong attached to satellites. Astronauts watch television monitors attached to the arm and control it accordingly through a series of switches. The first space repair mission the arm was involved in took place in April, 1984, when *Challenger* used the arm to pluck the malfunctioning Space Max satellite out of orbit. The satellite was pulled into the cargo bay of the shuttle, repaired by the crew, and then returned to orbit by Canadarm.

There are many unexplored frontiers here on earth that

provide further possible applications for Canadarm: the welding and repairing of pipelines on the ocean floor and the clean-up of radioactive and other hazardous wastes. In time we may not only be electrified by the spectacular performance of Canadarm in space, but also by how it performs for human needs on Earth.

SPEED OF SOUND

"Science is the slaying of a beautiful hypothesis by an ugly fact," says one definition. For forty-four years, scientists and engineers, indeed anyone who used the figure for the speed of sound, believed it to be 741.5 miles per hour, or 331.45 meters per second. It took a Canadian, Dr. George Wong, working in 1984 on the problem of calibrating microphones as accurately as possible, to find that this figure is slow by about a half mile per hour. Wong, whose findings were published in May, 1986, found that the original figure for the speed of sound was derived from an experiment done by Dr. H. C. Hardy in 1942. Dr. Hardy took his sample of air from "a light breeze of fresh outdoor air from a nearby window." He put the air through a purification process to remove the carbon dioxide. To arrive at the figure for the speed of sound in air, he made a numerical correction. As Dr. Wong says, "You know physicists, they always calculate things assuming this, assuming that. Unfortunately, he [Hardy] did not know how reliable his corrections were. And for the succeeding thirty years everybody who followed used his corrections. Nobody looked at how the first guy got it to start with."

Wong's figure for the speed of sound, 741.1 miles per hour or 331.29 meters per second in dry air, at zero degrees centigrade, standard air pressure at sea level (the international standard for air), does not make much difference for most engineering problems that deal with the speed of sound. But the difference is crucial in the area of maintaining standards, Dr. Wong's specialty, because distances measured within one-thousandth of an inch using the speed of sound and the measurement of properties in pure gases require the more accurate number.

This incredible level of accuracy takes us a long way from Newton's era, when experimenters would stand on hilltops and measure the time between the flash of a musket miles away and the arrival of the report, and try to figure out if it mattered which way the wind was blowing or whether the sound travelled uphill or downhill!

Since 1984, Dr. Wong's work has been followed more closely in the United States, Europe and Asia than in Canada. "There's an old Chinese proverb that says if you want to buy ginger for cooking you have to go to the next village. It takes outside people to recognize your work before you get recognition at home," Dr. Wong says. In May 1987, he received an award of merit from the education foundation of the Ontario Foundation of Chinese Canadian Professionals.

C F GENE DISCOVERY

A molecular biologist at the Hospital for Sick Children in Toronto, Ontario, Lap-Chee Tsui and a team of scientists working under him achieved a major breakthrough in July 1989 after a seven-year search. They discovered the gene carrying the defect that causes cystic fibrosis (CF), a disease that kills half of its victims by the time they are twenty-five years old and a large majority of them by the time they are thirty, and that affects one in two thousand Canadian children.

Tsui has likened the achievement to finding a single home in a city the size of Toronto without having an address or map. The search involved examining the estimated hundred thousand genes contained in the twenty-three chromosomes of each human cell and tracking the one gene that carried the defect. The next step for Tsui and his colleagues involves finding out what the defect is, information that it is hoped will lead to the ability to correct for the genetic defect and eliminate the symptoms of CF. This process could take years and requires working in unexplored regions of human cells, but for now Tsui's discovery at least allows for testing to determine who carries the defect, and whether it has been passed on from parent to child.

Safety

FIRST STEAM FOGHORN

Robert Foulis (1796-1866) was born in Glasgow, Scotland, and studied medicine, engineering, and painting there before emigrating to Canada in 1818. In 1821, he moved to St, John, New Brunswick, and while there he established the St. John Foundry, a "school of arts", and was a founding member of the Mechanics' Institute. He was working as a civil engineer during this time, and in 1853 he presented his design for a steam fog whistle to the Lighthouse Commissioners in New Brunswick. The first steam foghorn in the world was installed at Partridge Island, New Brunswick, in 1860, but it was not until a government report concerning his submission to the commissioners was published a few years later that Foulis was recognized as the inventor of the instrument.

Foulis' steam foghorn was a major contribution to marine safety that is still in use today. Lighthouses had been used for centuries but had not proven to be effective for warning ships of treacherous reefs in fog. In the mid-1800s large bells were in use, but they could not be heard over very great distances. Foulis' steam whistle, however, could be heard for miles and also sent out automatically coded blasts of sound, so that the navigator of a ship could tell from the pattern of short and long sounds exactly what piece of land the ship was near.

CRASH POSITION INDICATOR (C.P.I.)

Another Canadian contribution to international safety, the crash position indicator (C.P.I.), which floats away from an airplane about to crash, has saved many lives and become a vital part of aviation equipment. Today, the generic term for these devices is Emergency Locator Transmitter (ELT), and they are required equipment on all aircraft. Designed by Canadians Harry T. Stevinson and David M. Makow at the Radio and Electrical Engineering division of the National Research Council in 1959, the Canadian indicator was first manufactured by Leigh Instruments at Carleton Place, Ontario. Spar Aerospace Limited took over Leigh Instruments which went bankrupt in April 1990. Spar, a Canadian company, now handles sales of the C.P.I. worldwide. Because it makes immediate help more likely, Stevinson and Makow's invention prevents deaths caused by unattended injuries or exposure. It also decreases the search time for a downed plane, making it less likely that the search planes will have problems flying in conditions that caused the initial accident.

Although many attempts have been made to improve upon the idea of a crash position indicator, and there are several on the market today, nothing has come close to Stevinson and Makow's design. Over the years, the electronics, structural materials, and release mechanism of the C.P.I. have all been improved, but every modification has been based on the original principle of their design. The changes have meant that the cost and weight of the C.P.I. have decreased, while its reliability has improved.

The indicator weighs about six pounds and can be attached to small aircraft, which have the largest number of accidents. The design of the indicator, a radio beacon embedded in a piece of plastic foam shaped like a short section of an aircraft wing, has not changed. Originally, the indicator was attached to the tail of the aircraft by a slim metal ribbon passing through a spring loaded knife activated to cut the indicator free in the event of a change in tension resulting from a crash or other emergency. Now, an electrical switch mounted just inside the skin on the nose of the aircraft activates the mechanical release of the indicator, still attached to the tail of the aircraft, on impact. Helicopters often have a cockpit switch for the pilot to activate the release of the indicator. Another version releases the indicator if the craft is sinking in water, once the water pressure reaches a certain point.

Once released into the airstream, the indicator is lifted in a high arc and lands away from the the point of impact, due to its aerodynamic design. As it falls, it slows down so that it lands at a safe speed of about 40 miles (64.5 kilometers) per hour. Because of improvements in technology used in the indicator, it is adaptable to even greater variances in conditions than twenty-five years ago.

Other developments have added to the indicator's effectiveness. The SARSAT system, consisting of one U.S. and three Soviet satellites orbiting the earth, picks up signals from C.P.I.s and transmits them to central stations. After passing over twice, the satellite can pinpoint the location of a signal to within five miles. This has greatly aided search and rescue missions. As well, flight data recorders, introduced fifteen years ago, are now standard equipment, and aid researchers greatly in determining the cause of a crash. However, the effectiveness of the indicator and the data recorder depends on their surviving the crash. Leigh Instruments has embodied their data recorder into the C.P.I., greatly increasing the chances of recovering crucial flight information. In one hundred recorded crashes, the Canadian C.P.I. has deployed properly over ninety percent of the time. In one series of ten crashes since the data recorders were incorporated into the C.P.I., the flight information was recovered every time. The effectiveness of this system is crucial when a plane crashes into the sea. With the Canadian system, the indicator and flight recorder remain floating on the surface of the water, not under the water inside the plane. The millions of dollars spent in search of the flight recorder of KAL flight 007, that crashed into the North Pacific Ocean, is a case in point of how important it is to recover this information.

EXPLOSIVES VAPOUR DETECTOR

A recent Canadian innovation is one its creator hopes won't go over with a bang. Dr. Lorne Elias of the National Aeronautics Division of Canada's National Research Council spent eight years researching his invention. It's the first Explosives Vapour Detector (EVD) and is now in use in ten international airports in Canada—making theirs among the best security systems in the world—as well as in the United States, England, Denmark, Italy, and Germany. Elias says of his device, "EVD is the best of its type in the world, it's so sensitive that it can detect a concentration equal to one thimbleful of material present in Lake Superior." That is a sensitivity of one part of explosive material to one trillion parts of air.

Made up of two sections, the Explosives Vapour Detector

has a hand-held air sampler powered by an air pump that collects the samples in tiny glass cartridges that are then removed and connected to a portable suitcase-size analyzer unit. The device takes two and a half minutes to analyze the sample and register the presence of any explosive material; a digital display reads OK if no explosives are detected and ALARM if explosives are detected, with a number from 1 to 999 indicating the concentration of the material. After a detection is registered, dogs are usually brought in to pinpoint the material. Dr. Elias is working on a method to reduce the analysis time to five seconds.

The EVD is produced by Scintrex Limited in Concorde, Ontario, (near Toronto) and by Scintrex Incorporated in the United States. The company is developing a robot arm on a guided trolley to collect the samples in areas where an explosion is expected to take place and it would be too dangerous for a bomb squad to search for the explosive material. The arm would carry five sample cartridges, take the samples, then return them to the EVD for analysis. The company is also trying to open up the European market further to increase the security of European airports in the face of terrorism.

Art

FIRST NON-NATIVE THEATRICAL PRESENTATION IN NORTH AMERICA

Marc Lescarbot (c.1570-1642) was a French lawyer and writer who spent the winter of 1606-07 at the settlement of Port-Royal, in what is now Nova Scotia. He was a member of Samuel de Champlain's Ordre de Bon Temps (Order of Good Cheer—See First Social Club in North America) and involved in the meals and entertainment that each man in the Order provided to its members. During his lifetime he published a book of poems, and a history of New France. But he is known best for his masque (a play with music and dialogue) called *Le Théatre de Neptune en la Nouvelle-France* (The Theatre of Neptune in New France).

On September 5, 1606, Sieur de Poutrincourt (1557-1615) and de Champlain (c.1570-1635) left Port Royal and explored as far south as Martha's Vineyard before they returned on the fourteenth of November. They were greeted by a performance of Lescarbot's masque, the first non-native theatrical presentation in North America north of Mexico. It was performed on several small boats with a cast of eleven settlers. Thus, not only was the performance the first non-native theatrical presentation, it was also the first floating theatrical presentation and, given the mid-November climate, the performers must have thanked their lucky stars that they didn't step off the stage to join the sea god Neptune on the ocean's floor.

In 1962, a regional repertory theater opened in Halifax and was named the Neptune Theatre in honor of Lescarbot's pioneering performance. Productions of the play are still performed at the theater.

FIRSTS IN PHOTOGRAPHY AND MOTION PICTURES

Canada has had a lot of firsts in the field of photography, though the reasons are not as obvious as in the case of the pulp and paper industry. Many of the pioneering achievements in photography in Canada seem to have been inspired by a desire to understand the diverse land mass and cultures that make up Canada through the medium of photography and motion pictures.

First panoramic camera

First of all, Canada produced the first panoramic camera, still in general use today. Patented in 1887 by John Connon of Elora, Ontario, the apparatus was made to revolve on a tripod, giving a continuous 360 degree picture, without splices, less expensively and more accurately than the old multiple-exposure camera. The camera seemed particularly useful to photograph large groups, except for the unexpected behavior that it caused. Apparently, especially when students were being photographed, people would stand at one end of the group as the camera began to photograph, and then run around to other end to get in the picture twice. As they ran the people in the center would naturally turn to watch them, and the back of their heads would be immortalized on film.

First portable film developing system

A few years later, in December 1890, Arthur Williams McCurdy received a Canadian and U.S. patent for "an apparatus for developing flexible photographic film." As with many other Canadian inventions, McCurdy's portable box was not marketed in Canada. He sold his patents in 1903 to George Eastman of Rochester, New York, who in turn sold the device under the name of "Kodak Developing Machines," to go along with his Kodak camera.

First documentary film

The first documentary film was produced in Canada. Many people have seen *Nanook of the North* during their school days, but few realize that this was the first film ever termed a "documentary." Produced, directed and filmed by Robert Flaherty, an American, in 1920 and 1921 in northern Ungava, the film helped cultivate a better understanding of those who live in the harsh northern regions of North America by the people in the friendlier climes of the continent. The film also set a style and standard for subsequent real-life features. The subject of the film, Nanook, (the name means "the Bear") was an actual hunter whom Flaherty befriended in the eastern Arctic. Nanook died in 1924, two years after the film was released.

Documentary film making has not only become an important aspect of our education, allowing television to be more than just an entertainment forum, it has also become a world industry, recording aspects of culture and the natural world that otherwise might be lost forever.

First commercial motion picture

The first commercial picture, indeed probably the first film advertisement in the world, was made by James Freer, a Manitoban farmer, in the fall of 1897. The film depicted life on the prairies and was used in 1898 and 1899 in the United Kingdom to promote immigration to Canada.

First deluxe movie theater

The first "deluxe" motion picture theater in the world, with upholstered seats rather then kitchen chairs, was opened by Leo Ernest Ouimet in 1907 on Ste. Catherine Street in Montreal. Ouimet charged the then outrageous price of ten to fifteen cents a seat, with reserved seats for twenty-five cents, at a time when most people were able to pay five cents to see a movie at a Nickelodeon. The movie house was called The Ouimetoscope.

First motion picture showing in North America

Two Canadians were responsible for the first motion picture showing in North America. According to a letter from Thomas Edison to George and Andrew Holland, two brothers who worked as photographers in Ottawa, the two Canadians opened the first Kinetoscope Parlour in the world in New York City in 1894. "Kinetoscope" machines allowed individuals to view motion pictures. This date precedes all other accounts of film showings, and though it may not have been the absolute first, it was certainly one of the earliest.

FIRST ELECTRONIC WAVE ORGAN

The first in a generation of instruments that produce sound electronically, the first electronic organ to be demonstrated to the public and press, and to be manufactured and sold commercially was invented by Frank Morse Robb of Belleville, Ontario. In 1927, when he was 24, Robb recorded the natural wave form of the sound of an organ at the Bridge Street United Church in Belleville. After photographing the wave forms that were created on an oscillograph, he reproduced them on metal disks which produced a series of impulses when tracked by an electromagnetic pick-up head. When the impulses were amplified the recorded tones were duplicated. Robb obtained a Canadian patent for his invention in 1928, seven years before any other electronic organs were produced in the world.

Failing in his search to find a Canadian company to produce the organ, and rather than sell his idea to a company in the United States, Robb set up his own company in Belleville in 1934, the Robb Wave Organ Company. By 1936, he had delivered his first organs to stores and chapels in the Toronto area. But his timing could not have been worse for entering into such an entrepreneurial project, the stock market had crashed in 1929 and by 1936 the depression was in full swing. People were not willing to buy the organs, let alone invest in the struggling company. Discouraged, Robb suffered a nervous breakdown in 1937, and his company folded.

However, he left his mark on the history of music forever. The Hammond Organ Company, which produced its first true electronic organ in 1939, was selling $300 million worth of electronic organs by 1965 (Hammond was taken over by Crabbe Holdings of Sydney, Australia, in 1986). The variation in musical sound produced electronically today, still by replicating wave forms of traditional instruments, as Robb did first, would have amazed and delighted the inventor of the electronic wave organ.

SUPERMAN

It's a bird! It's a plane! It's Canadian! Superman, "the world's most famous comic-book hero", was created by Canadian Joe Shuster, a Toronto Star newspaper artist and American Jerome Siegel. The comic first appeared in June 1938. In the strip, Clark Kent's newspaper was first called *The Daily Star*. The name was changed to *The Daily Planet* only when the strip became syndicated on a wider scale. Shuster and Siegel sold their rights to the character to DC Comics in 1940.

Ironically, in a 1986 issue, *Time* magazine listed Superman, a partly Canadian creation, as a symbol of the strength and greatness of the United States. In *Superman*, the movie, Canadians became involved once again: Quebec-born Glenn Ford played Superman's adoptive father, and Yellowknife (NWT)-born Margot Kidder played Clark Kent's girlfriend, Lois Lane. The fiftieth anniversary of Superman's appearance was celebrated in 1988 with a special float in the Macy's Thanksgiving Parade; a CBS Television Salute; and in Cleveland, where Superman was created, a tickertape parade, the unveiling of a statue, a permanent Superman exhibition, and a major comic convention.

NATIONAL FILM BOARD— World Leader in Documentary Films

The word "documentary" is first applied to film; NFB's first Oscar-winning film

The National Film Board of Canada (known as NFB and in French as ONF—Office National du Film) was founded on May 2, 1939, by the National Film Act of Parliament. The NFB was created as a public production agency "to promote the production and distribution of films in the nation and in particular... to interpret

Canada to Canadians and to other countries." The pioneer documentary filmmaker John Grierson (1898-1972) was invited by the Canadian government to come from Britain to serve as the first Government Film Commissioner and survey the situation. As the first person to apply the word "documentary" to film (when describing a film by Robert Flaherty), Grierson's influence in the early years laid the foundation of the Board's reputation as a leader in the production of documentary films. In 1941, Stuart Legg's documentary *Churchill's Island* won the Board's first Hollywood Oscar. This was the first time an Oscar was given to a documentary film.

Norman McLaren—originator of animation techniques

In 1941, Grierson invited a young artist named Norman McLaren (1914-87) to set up the animation unit of the Board. Since then, both McLaren and the work of the Board have been renowned for their contributions to the industry. McLaren was a master of animation and one of the first to experiment with and popularize optical printing and drawing directly on film. He was also the originator of animating soundtracks, known for his stop-motion cinematography called "pixillation", and maker of one of the few existing three-dimensional animated films.

NFB's Candid Eye Series

In the late 1950s, the National Film Board's Candid Eye series emerged. Using light-weight camera and sound equipment, film crews were able to follow the subjects of the film and allow them to speak for themselves. Crews of one or two persons could film police on actual cases, or the young Canadian singing star Paul Anka struggling through a crowd of fans. The immediacy and intimacy of these films revolutionized the use of film for television in Canada and the United States and was the world's first use of direct cinema.

World's largest government film unit

The quality of the National Film Board's work and its contribution to the film industry has been recognized worldwide. New York's Museum of Modern Art ran a major retrospective, in 1981, of over three hundred NFB films, covering all aspects of the animation, documentary and feature film work. In 1979, the NFB's fortieth anniversary was celebrated across Canada and the Academy of Motion Picture Arts paid a special tribute to the NFB in "recognition of forty years of superior artistry in motion pictures and of leading the way in the development of documentary film."

The NFB is the world's largest government film unit and since its inception it has won almost three thousand national and international awards, more than any other film unit in Canada, including three Palmes d'Or from Cannes and five Robert Flaherty awards. Fifty-five NFB films have been nominated for Academy Awards and nine have won. In 1989, the Board celebrated its fiftieth anniversary and received a special commemorative Palmes d'Or and Academy Award in honor of its achievements.

Studio D—The only woman's English film studio in the world

Although most of the Board's productions have been documentaries, more than thirty feature films have been produced wholly by the Board and dozens more have been coproduced by the Board providing some funding. Today the NFB has an entire studio devoted primarily to the production of dramatic films. The head office of the NFB is in Ottawa; the main production studios are in Montreal. The Board's most influential studio, and the studio with the highest profile over the past ten years, is Studio D, headed by Virginia Stikeman, which concentrates on producing films for women and from a woman's perspective. Two of Studio D's films have been especially notable over the past few years: *Not A Love Story*, directed by Bonnie Klein, presented a controversial look at pornography and helped make its subject a national issue in Canada; and *If You Love This Planet*, directed by Terri Nash, won an Academy Award. The latter was labelled "political propaganda" by the U.S. Justice Department and has become an important part of the anti-nuclear campaign. Studio D, which is the only women's English film studio in the world, celebrated its fifteenth anniversary in 1989. A French women's studio was set up at the NFB in Montreal in 1986.

I MAX FILM FORMAT

In 1949, Colin Low of Cardston, Alberta, joined the National Film Board (NFB) as a graphic artist. By 1959, he had become involved in filmmaking, trained in this new profession by NFB's master animator, Norman McLaren. In the 1960s, Low helped develop revolutionary film formats in the film industry. One of the projects he was involved in was codirecting the spectacular film *Labyrinth* for the 1967 World Exposition in Montreal. *Labyrinth* used both 70-mm and 35-mm film and was projected on several screens, giving the viewer ten times the information that normal films do. This film was the precursor to the IMAX and OMNIMAX film formats now used in many amusement park films and documentaries.

In 1968, Grahame Ferguson, Roman Kroitor and Robert Kerr invented IMAX ("I" for eye plus "MAX" for maximum—the most the eye can see) motion pictures for the Canadian pavilion at Expo 1970 in Osaka, Japan. The first permanent IMAX theater, Cinesphere, opened that same year at Ontario Place, on Toronto's waterfront. There are now ten permanent IMAX theaters in the United States, and fifty-five others in fourteen countries around the world. IMAX uses 70-mm film turned sideways, the largest film frame in history, producing six-storey-high projected images. The films are produced by IMAX Systems Corporation of Toronto, and the specially designed IMAX film projectors are built in Oakville, Ontario. Two of the documentaries filmed with IMAX cameras are *Hail Columbia* and *The Dream is Alive*, both of which captured the launch of the NASA Space Shuttle. Other IMAX films include *Transitions*, made for Expo 1986 in Vancouver, B.C., and *The Heart*, both of which were directed by Colin Low and Tony Ianzelo, with cameraman Ernest McNabb.

Imax Systems Corporation unveiled its new Solido system in Spring 1990. The new system involves three-dimensional images which are projected upon a dome shaped screen seventy-nine feet (twenty-four meters) in diameter that is tilted to fill the audience's full field of vision from side to side and above. The experience of watching films in such a theater has been likened to looking and moving around in real visual space. As Roman Kroitor stated at the screening of a demonstration film, "When you're experiencing a

Solido film, where the dome-like screen occupies all of the retina, it feels very different. The more of your retina that's occupied by the image, the more powerful it is psychologically."

CANADA COUNCIL

The Canada Council was established by Parliament in 1957 as an independent body to encourage the arts, humanities, and social sciences. With funds from the federal government, the Council gives fellowships and grants to individuals and arts organizations in the performing arts, writing, and publishing fields. It is unique in North America in its scope as a publicly funded arts supporter. This is partially a result of the difference between the political traditions of Canada and the United States. In Canada the government is much more involved in funding cultural programs, though the Canada Council is a statutory foundation, modeled on American foundations. In the United States the tradition has been to leave support of the arts to private donors.

The Council also serves several other functions: advising the government on cultural concerns, maintaining the Canadian commission for the United Nations Educational, Scientific, and Cultural Organization (UNESCO), administering the Governor General's Awards for Literature, and other honors. The current director of the Council, since January 1989, is Joyce Zemans.

PRISON ARTS FOUNDATION

The Prison Arts Foundation of Canada is the first volunteer organization in the world to promote creative activity programs in prisons and to show prison art in an exhibition that toured nationwide. Though not a large organization, the Foundation has made a tremendous difference in the lives of those it has involved and touched. Many inmates have found a way to communicate with the world, benefiting in a purely personal way in the act of learning to create something and to express themselves, and in doing so freeing themselves. The most well known artists to come out of this program are probably Michel Pellus and Pierre Dupuis. Pellus began his career as an artist while in prison and has gone on to painting sets for Les Grands Ballets Canadiens and designing posters for the St. Jean Baptiste Day celebrations in Quebec. Dupuis graduated from university in Quebec and is doing very well as an artist. One of his works is currently on loan to Government House, home of Canada's governor general.

The Foundation was established in 1967, as a result of a Christmas card contest sponsored by a small volunteer organization for prison inmates. The competition was so successful that it became a regular event and was expanded to include all art forms, including literature and music. Incorporated in 1972, the Foundation is supported by the federal government and private donations and includes all inmates and parolees in the country. Its exhibition of inmates' art now tours across Canada. More than one million people see the exhibition each year and during the tour works are offered for sale on behalf of the inmates. Most of the exhibitions are held in shopping malls, but some are held in the prisons themselves. In 1975, the Foundation assembled the first international collection of prison arts and crafts from thirteen countries, including Canada.

The Prison Arts Foundation also sponsors workshops taught by artists for inmates in some prisons, but attendance is voluntary and the workshops are not connected to the prison system. Other than this means of contacting artists in prison, the Foundation leaves it up to the artist to approach the Foundation or enter art contests. Works that are entered into contests are judged by eminent Canadians in appropriate artistic fields. Each artist receives a positive critique of her or his work whether they win in their contest category or not. Winners receive cash awards ranging from $25 to $250.

ART BANK

Set up in 1972 by the Canada Council as an innovative way to assist artists, the Art Bank was the first of its kind. Since 1972, similar institutions have been established in Australia, Alaska, Santa Monica, California, Florida and several provinces of Canada. The Art Bank supplements support of artists through Canada Council grants by purchasing their work and making it available to the public. The aim of the Art Bank is to present contemporary Canadian art to the public and thereby stimulate the private and corporate collecting of art. Works by living, professional artists who are either Canadian citizens or have lived in Canada for five years are bought by the Art Bank and then rented for display to Canadian government departments, agencies, nonprofit organizations, schools and hospitals. At any given time about 70 percent of the works are rented out; the balance of the collection is stored and displayed in a warehouse. Annual rental fees total $750,000, enough to cover the cost of the program, allowing the Art Bank to use government funds to purchase art works.

The Art Bank does not initiate contact with the artists; the artists must request that their works be considered for purchase. Works to be purchased are selected by a jury whose members are selected by the director of the Art Bank. The jury is made up of respected members of the visual arts community who travel to each region of the country to consider works to be purchased. As of September 1985, the Bank had purchased twelve thousand works by more than 1,580 artists. The collection is broadly representative of the various tendencies in Canadian art since 1970 and it covers a full range of media. Public galleries often borrow from the Art Bank and its works have been in exhibitions around the world: in Paris, London, Australia and New Zealand.

The effectiveness of the Bank has been felt in another way. William Kirby, present director of the Art Bank, has noticed that many of the people who come into contact with the Art Bank do not necessarily know anything about art, let alone contemporary Canadian art. Many of them are simply interested in decorating their offices and come looking for a painting to match a couch or rug. Kirby makes it clear that the Art Bank is not a decorating service and by the time a person has gone through the process of selecting a work and living with it for a year or more, he or she has not only become attached to it but also learned a lot about Canadian art.

CHILDREN'S THEATER

When one asks Canadians to name Canadian activities they are proud of, more often than not they mention children's theater, that is, theater for young audiences. A relatively new art form and one developed by Canadians, it has grown in scope and excellence over the past decade and has achieved international acclaim. Since 1976, the number of professional companies devoted to theater for young audiences has more than doubled, and so has the possibility for training and the available materials on the subject. This remarkable growth is marked by the fact that Young People's Theatre (YPT) since 1977 has had its own building in Toronto, the only facility of its kind in Canada devoted exclusively to plays for young people. With this building, YPT is enabled to maintain high standards, attract top Canadian actresses and actors to appear in its productions, provide backstage tours, and offer a theater school and other related activities to children.

Canadian children's theater companies and productions have become cultural ambassadors for Canada. In the past decade there has been a shift from plays that focus on history and nationalism to plays that deal with specific contemporary problems. The specific goal of some of the companies is to provide "children with the tools to cope better with a world that has become increasingly confusing and complex." Theater for the young has always been a vehicle to carry valued traditions from one generation to the next, but recently the emphasis has been on dealing with issues of health, welfare and social unease. The balance between didactic drama and theater art is delicate and one with which the companies struggle. The present tours of elementary and high schools in Southern Ontario often contain plays concerning social action, wit and innocence that provoke varying reactions among the young audiences. For instance, city and country children audiences react differently to the production of Deverell's *Melody Meets the Bag Lady*, which may be indicative of the perceived threat strangers pose to city kids.

In the former Soviet Union and other eastern European countries, theater for the young was well subsidized. In western societies, Canada is unusual in its emphasis on theater for the young, and children's theater enjoys much greater funding than in the United States. Children today are beset by anxieties related to more than specific familial or social problems, and while theater for the young does not offer solutions to these problems, it does have the value of making young people conscious of the world around them such that they feel empowered to address their choices and responsibilities.

Business

FIRSTS IN PULP AND PAPER

Canada's largest industry, that of pulp and paper, is also its best known business, both in the United States and worldwide. It is not surprising, then, that Canada can lay claim to many firsts in this field. What few people know, however, is that its origins come from the lowly wasp.

In 1838, according to the claims of many Maritimers, Charles Fenerty (1821-92) of Halifax, Nova Scotia, had discovered a process of making paper from wood fiber. He came upon the idea while watching wasps chew wood fibers to make their nests. Fenerty began experimenting in 1839 and produced his paper from sprucewood pulp, through either mechanical or chemical means. His firm, white paper was apparently exhibited in 1844.

The authenticity of Fenerty's achievement remains in dispute. That it is, nevertheless, a Canadian first is less uncertain. In the mid-1800s the U.S. Civil War had caused a great shortage of rags and cloth and, since paper was often made from rags, a shortage of paper occurred. John Thomson of Napanee, Ontario, set his mind to the search for a substitute for cloth or rag paper and wood pulp made by grinding the wood. In 1864, he made the first chemical wood pulp by boiling the wood chips under pressure with chemicals. In 1869, Alex Buntin imported grinders from Germany and used them to set up the first commercial mechanical pulp mill in North America at Valleyfield, Quebec, near Montreal.

In the late 1800s, the pulp and paper industry grew rapidly in Canada. U.S. newspapers, in order to ensure a continuous supply of newsprint, set up plants of their own or made loans to Canadian companies so that they could expand their paper-making operations. The first plant in North America to manufacture kraft paper (used for wrapping and making packing and cardboard boxes) was the Brompton (Quebec) Pulp and Paper Company at East Angus, started in 1907. That year the Brompton company also built the first mill in North America to produce chemical pulp by the sulphate or draft process in East Angus. Canada also has the only paper-making school in North America at Trois-Rivières, Quebec.

F ULLER BRUSH COMPANY

Alfred C. Fuller (1885-1973), called the "father of door-to-door sales," was born in Welsford, Nova Scotia. When times got rough at home, he moved to Hartford, Connecticut, to live with his sister. Working out of his sister's basement in 1906, Fuller began making brushes at night and selling them door-to-door during the day. Thus, from the depths of the cellar and the innovation of this twenty-one-year-old Canadian, the legendary Fuller Brush man was born.

By the fifties and sixties, the Fuller Brush had become a household word. Fuller's credo proved true: "With equal opportunity to all and due consideration for each person involved in every transaction, a business must succeed." Two popular Hollywood movies were based on his company, so appealing was the image created. The first movie, *The Fuller Brush Man*, starred Red Skelton; the other was *The Fuller Brush Woman*, with Lucille Ball. Today most of the dealers for the company are women. Its headquarters are back in Canada, at Brantford, Ontario.

Trying to regain some of its earlier popularity, the company relies heavily on historical familiarity. One of the Brantford salespersons reports that the Fuller Brush image still serves them well: "I've never worked for a company selling door-to-door where people actually want to buy the product. . . . Yuppies in Toronto buy brushes out of nostalgia for the Fuller Brush Man. They buy one just so they can say that they own a Fuller Brush."

DEVELOPMENT OF PROCESS FOR PRODUCING CALCIUM CARBIDE AND ACETYLENE GAS

In 1892, Thomas L. "Carbide" Willson (1860-1915) of Woodstock, Ontario, developed the first commercial process for the production of calcium carbide and acetylene gas. He discovered the process at Spray, North Carolina, while experimenting in the laboratory at his business, the Willson Aluminum Co. The substance, a greyish-black, lumpy, crystalline powder, is usually produced through a reaction between anthracite and limestone or quicklime.

He returned to Canada in the 1890s. He obtained over seventy patents in Canada and patented several marine devices that used acetylene. His development of the process for producing calcium carbide laid the basis for the development of the electro-chemical industry. The sale of his process and patents led to the founding of the Union Carbide Company of the United States, while Willson became the first vice-president of the Shawnigan Chemical Company back in Canada. In 1903, the invention of the oxyacetylene torch turned out to be the most important use of acetylene, useful not only in welding but also in steel-cutting and all other metalwork in the ship-building and automobile industry.

THE ZIPPER

In 1925, Swedish-born inventor Gideon Sundback came to Canada and became the president of Lightning Fastener Company of St. Catharines, Ontario. About fifteen years earlier Sundback had furthered work on an idea originally conceived by an American, Whitcomb L. Judson, a portly gentleman who had experienced trouble fastening his boots with either buttons or laces. Judson had patented a "slide fastener" in 1891 and 1893 and, together with Colonel Louis Walker, founded the Universal Fastener Company, later the Hook and Eye Company, of Hoboken, New Jersey.

Judson and Walker, looking to improve both the design and manufacturing machinery for their invention, hired Gideon Sundback, an engineer who had been working for Westinghouse Electric in Pittsburgh, Pennsylvania. Sundback had already shown a great interest in the fastener. His research led to a dramatic departure from the hook and eye models already tried. What he invented became known as the "zipper"—originally the trade name for rubber galoshes made by the B. F. Goodrich Company and equipped with the new hookless fasteners. He received his U.S. patent for the invention on April 29, 1913, and it was originally marketed as the Talon Slide Fastener. Later the name of the galoshes became used for the fastener itself.

Sundback's claim to the invention and the Canadian patent were legally challenged in 1934, but were upheld by the Privy Council of Canada, establishing Sundback as the inventor of the zipper.

PAINT ROLLER

Unless you aspire to paint your ceiling as Michelangelo did the Sistine Chapel, you are probably familiar with and grateful for the humble paint roller. A godsend to painters and decorators all over the world, the paint roller was invented in 1940 by Norman Breakey of Toronto.

Typical of Canadian inventors even to the present, Breakey was unable to partake in the financial bonanza that resulted from his simple invention. Unable to persuade Canadians to risk their capital, Breakey had no backing for the development of his invention. To add insult to injury, he couldn't afford to defend the patent from infringement. Consequently, although he revolutionized the painting and decorating industry and helped introduce do-it-yourself decorating, Breakey died in modest circumstances.

AUTOMATIC CONTROL OF MACHINE TOOLS

In 1945, Canadian Eric W. Leaver (born in 1915) began researching the possible uses of technology developed during World War II in industry. He focused upon the problems that had to be solved in order to build a functional "hand-arm machine," as he called it. By mid-1946, he had developed a system he called Automatic Machine Control by Recorded Operation (AMCRO), and in the November 1946 issue of *Fortune* magazine Leaver published an article entitled "The Automatic Factory." The article set out Leaver's ideas and illustrations of a fully automated factory. What Leaver had developed and began to build in a small Toronto plant with the help of Canadian engineer G. R. Mounce was the first production tool that could be programmed to repeat the operations of a worker making a product, the forerunner of the automated systems found in many factories today.

AMCRO was in operation in Leaver's Toronto plant in 1947, and people came from around the world to see it. The machine was attached to a nine-inch lathe and recorded the tool's position and speed as a worker made a sample part. The recording could then be played back, in effect "telling" the lathe how to turn the stock piece into a finished part. Leaver's system was only one of many ways that were developed later to control machine tools automatically. Though they had tried and rejected many other systems before settling on AMCRO, Leaver and Mounce were only able to patent the one system. As a result they were not able to protect the basic idea under their exclusive ownership. Nevertheless, Leaver's company, Electronic Associates, went on to produce electronic instruments and had more than $15 million of business in 1974 when he lost control of it. It has been estimated that if they had been able to protect and to develop their idea fully, it would have been the largest money-making innovation in the history of Canadian technology. The numerous developments in automated production processes today support this claim.

GREEN GARBAGE BAG

The plastic garbage bag was conceived, tested, and first marketed in Canada. There are actually two stories about the first bag ever. One begins in Winnipeg after World War II, where the Wasylyk family owned a fruit and vegetable canning company. After the war price controls were lifted and the price of tin increased rapidly, putting the Wasylyk's canning company out of business. One of the newest things around was polyethylene, and Harry Wasylyk started a brand new packaging business in his kitchen making bags for fruits and vegetables. He did very well at this and was soon out of his kitchen producing the bags and selling them to produce stores and industrial plants around the city. But there was another, and soon to be more important, client. Wasylyk's company was also selling polyethylene surgical gloves to the Winnipeg General Hospital. Hospital officials told Harry of the problem they had keeping the garbage cans they used sanitary. As a result, he developed the plastic garbage bag to line the garbage cans; when it was full, it would be thrown out with the garbage.

The second story involves Harry's competitor, the giant corporation Union Carbide which was manufacturing polyethylene in Lindsay, Ontario, at the same time Harry was running his plant in Winnipeg. According to the Carbide workers, the plant manager at the time, Larry Hanson, was also making plastic garbage bags and hand sealing them himself at the plant for use at his cottage and cleaning up around the plant. Both men were producing the bag in the early 1950s, although it is still unclear who began first.

However, Union Carbide bought Harry Wasylyk's business, including the bags he was selling to the hospital, so that it now had three plants in Canada, in Lindsay, Winnipeg and in Montreal. Union Carbide was at the time the largest producer of polyethylene resin in the British Empire and John Morley was given the job of coming up with a product that would use the eleven million pounds of polyethylene resin Union Carbide had in Montreal. After viewing product lines at the three plants, Morley felt that the only product that would possibly use up the material, and then only if it sold really well, was the garbage bag that the Winnipeg General Hospital and a few industrial plants were using. The bags had been tested only in these several places, but had been praised for working very well for garbage cleanups. So Union Carbide went with the product and Morley set about promoting it with the slogan "Ban the Can and Save Your Man."

However, in municipalities across the country the bags were illegal; garbage had to be put out in cans. Finally, Morley convinced the city of Etobicoke, Ontario, to give the bags a test, and once it agreed, he ensured the success of the test by preceding the garbage collectors on their route and re-wrapping any bags that had been punctured or torn by rodents or other animals. However, the market for the bags, then called "Polybag garbage bags", didn't increase that much and by 1967 they were still available only in hardware stores. The turning point was coming up though.

Union Carbide owned the Canadian rights to Glad products, and the company was looking for an extension to the Glad product line of sandwich bags and plastic wrap. In 1969, Bob Rastorp was the man who decided to promote a new line of bags as "Glad garbage bags." After obtaining permission from the Glad head office in New York which told Union Carbide that no one would pay for something they were going to throw away, they brought the "Man from Glad" up from the States for advertisements and started selling the bags in the large chain stores.

The bags sold well, although people called the company and complained that the garbage collectors kept taking their bags away, instead of emptying them and leaving them for the house-holder to use again. When they were introduced in the United States, the business expanded at an incredible rate. In 1986, the Home Products Division of Union Carbide, including Glad products, was bought out by First Brands Corporation based in Toronto and a subsidiary of First Brands Corporation of Danbury, Connecticut. The bags are now manufactured at a plant in Orangeville, Ontario. In 1991, 732 million bags were sold in Canada, totalling $84.4 million that year in retail, and about eighty percent of families in Canada now use them.

TRIVIAL PURSUITS AND OTHER BOARD GAMES

Just when we were getting bored and didn't feel like resorting to Monopoly once again, two Canadians rescued us. In 1982, few people in the United States had heard of "Trivial Pursuit"; now it is rare to find someone who hasn't played it. Bars have proclaimed Trivial Pursuit nights, there are radio shows based on it, and fund-raising programs have used the idea. Best of all, the game has given a good time to millions of people around the world, inviting discussion, involvement and reaction.

"A Party in a Box" proclaimed a *New York Times* article when the rage first hit. One of the inventors, Chris Haney, was stopped in the street by a rather heavy-set man who asked him if he was the Chris Haney. When Haney answered yes, the man gave him a big hug and said, "That's the most fun I've ever had!" Haney had to agree: he and his co-inventor, Scott Abbott, both in their mid-thirties, are now millionaires. In 1983, sales of Trivial Pursuit outstripped traditional games like "Scrabble" and "Monopoly."

The game was conceived on December 5, 1979, in an argument between the two over who was the better Scrabble player. Haney went out to buy the game and realized that it was the sixth game of Scrabble he had bought in his life. So Haney, photo editor of the *Montreal Gazette*, and Abbott, a sportswriter for *Canadian Press*, decided to invent their own board game. "It took us 45 minutes to design the game and three months to figure out the scoring," says Abbott.

Neither had any marketing experience, so they went to a Canadian Toy and Decoration fair in Montreal in January 1980, posing as a photographer and journalist and intending to get all the information they could from toy manufacturers about the strategies of marketing a game. They collected about ten thousand dollar's worth of information in that one afternoon, according to Abbott. They decided to start their own company, Horn Abbott Limited. Haney quit his job and went to Spain with his family, his brother, and a pile of almanacs, encyclopedias, guides and record books. There he and his family worked solidly for about a month collecting mounds of trivia. When he returned to Canada, he and Abbott coerced, teased and begged thirty-two friends to give them enough money to produce the first twelve hundred test-market copies in the fall of 1981. It was rough going at first, but finally, in March 1982, they received a loan and began to produce the game. By October their four man assembly line couldn't keep up with the demand so they gave the distribution rights for Canada over to Chieftain Products. In the United States in 1982, they licensed Selchow and Righter Company (taken over in 1986 by Coleco) for manufacturing and distribution of the game. Coleco, while battling bankruptcy, lost the rights to manufacture the game in 1988 and since January 1989 the manufacturing rights to the game for Canada and the United States have been owned by Tonka Corporation of Minnesota.

There's nothing trivial about the numbers. The investment of the original private shareholders increased twenty-five times and there were once more than one thousand Canadians involved in manufacturing the game and getting it to the markets. Now that Tonka Corporation manufactures the game, all production is done in the United States by Parker Brothers, a division of Tonka. By 1987, worldwide retail sales had reached two billion dollars. Over fifty million games have been sold worldwide, thirty-eight million in North America alone. The game is sold in thirty countries outside of North

America and produced in sixteen languages. Recently, Horn Abbott International, which owns the rights to the game for everywhere except North America, has been involved in negotiations to distribute the game in China and the Soviet Union. There are now a hundred versions of the game, including the Genus original edition, Genus II edition, the Silver Screen edition, the All Star Sports edition, the Baby Boomer edition, the Disney edition, a Young Players edition, a Juniors edition, as well as six Mini-editions. Pocket Packs, which come with one hundred and twenty cards and a hand-held scoring card, have also been introduced recently.

Trivial Pursuit was not the first Canadian board game to meet with such huge success. In the late 1800s, a wealthy Canadian couple created a game they called "The Yacht Game." Their friends enjoyed playing it so much on their yacht that they suggested they try to sell it to others. In the 1920s, the couple sold the rights to the game to Edwin S. Lowe, who was then famous for selling bingo games, and he changed the name to the now familiar "Yachtzee." In 1973, Hasbro Canada (with its Milton Bradley product line) bought out E.S.Lowe Ltd. and now owns the rights to the game, of which forty million copies have been sold to date.

Between Yachtzee and Trivial Pursuit, however, there was not that much activity in board game inventing in Canada. However, other board games have followed Trivial Pursuit's lead out of Canada into the United States and worldwide. In 1984, Canada Games Company of Downsview, Ontario, introduced "Balderdash," invented by Laura Robinson, a Canadian actress, and Paul Toyne, both of whom are from Toronto, Ontario. It shipped the millionth game in Canada in 1990, and two and a half million copies have been sold worldwide to date totalling about forty million dollars in sales. In 1986, Canada Games introduced "An Evening of Murder," invented by Max Hanes, Toronto newspaper crime reporter, and since then it has sold five hundred thousand copies in Canada alone. And in July 1989, the company introduced Humzinger, a game invented by Torontonians Jerry Kuleba and Joe Shyllit, which sold sixty-five thousand copies in Canada by December 1989.

"Supremacy," another game introduced in 1984, and invented by Robert Simpson of Toronto, has sales totalling sixty-five thousand copies and three million dollars to date. In 1986, Trivial Pursuit was outsold as Americans bought 1.6 million copies of the game, "A Question of Scruples," a card game involving personal morality that was invented by Henry Makow, a Winnipeg freelance writer and former part-time university professor. Since being introduced in 1985, seven million copies of Scruples have been sold worldwide. Makow still manufactures the game in Canada with the company High Game Enterprises, but the international rights were sold to Milton Bradley Company in 1985.

"Pictionary" was also invented by a Canadian, Rob Angel from Vancouver, British Columbia, though he was living in the United States at the time. The game was introduced in June 1986 and has sold fifteen million copies worldwide to date. Other Canadian successes in board games include "Ultimatum," invented by Fred Bates of Bates Games in Hamilton, Ontario, and introduced in 1985 it has sold 150,000 copies to date in Canada, the United States, Britain and Australia. Bates Games also introduced "Batman" in 1989, which has sold about five hundred thousand copies in Canada and the United States to date. In total, the games industry had sales of about sixty-five million dollars in Canada in 1989, and the future looks promising, with games such as "Rockstar," a board game by GIG Enterprises of Toronto, introduced in 1991.

FIRSTS AND FOREMOSTS IN UNDERSEA TECHNOLOGY

Deep Rover—most advanced single-person submarine in the world

The "Deep Rover" was built as part of a joint venture between Can-Dive Services, based in Vancouver, British Columbia and Deep Ocean Engineering of Oakland, California. The impetus for the project came from Petro-Canada (then a government-owned oil company in Canada). Designed in California, Deep Rover was built by Can-Dive in Dartmouth, Nova Scotia, at a cost of one million dollars in 1984. It is the most advanced single-person submarine in the world. Only one has been built to date.

An acrylic sphere that is best described as an "underwater helicopter," Deep Rover can dive to a depth of about 0.6 miles (914 meters). The average dive lasts four to six hours, but the sub has an emergency life-support system that lasts one week if necessary. Sea-level air pressure is maintained in the sub even at the

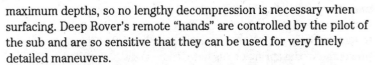

maximum depths, so no lengthy decompression is necessary when surfacing. Deep Rover's remote "hands" are controlled by the pilot of the sub and are so sensitive that they can be used for very finely detailed maneuvers.

Though the Deep Rover was rented by Petro-Canada between 1984 and 1985 for use at drilling rigs off Newfoundland, it has also been used extensively for marine science expeditions and marine construction.

The NEWTSUIT

The NEWTSUIT is a lightweight, one-atmosphere diving suit initially designed and developed by Phil Nuytten, president of Can-Dive Services and International Hardsuits, both located in Vancouver, British Columbia. The suit, which weighs about seven hundred pounds, can be used in depths of about half a mile (700 meters) and the use of a unique and revolutionary joint design allows the diver to move with about 75 percent the dexterity of a diver in a regular wetsuit. About ten suits have been built to date and sold to the Canadian Navy, Japan, Germany, the United States and the U.S. Navy for ocean-floor work in offshore oil and gas operations, military operations, and commercial diving outfits. International Hardsuits is currently involved in developing a thruster pack to allow the diver to move to different depths underwater, and a lightweight (hundred-pound; 220 kilogram) free-swimming suit for use at depths up to three hundred feet (91.44 meters).

Other developments

Two others have won Manning Awards for their contributions to undersea technology. In 1987, Dr. James R. McFarlane of International Submarine Engineering (I.S.E.) in Port Coquitlam, B.C., won a Manning Award of Merit for his contributions to the design and manufacture of underwater vehicles. In 1989, Donald Knudsen of Knudsen Engineering Ltd. in Perth, Ontario, won a Manning Award of Distinction for developing a high-resolution active sonar called "DAISY" (for Digital Acoustic Imaging System). The Sonar is considered to be the world's first practical underwater acoustic imaging system because it provides rapid, high-resolution visual images of underwater objects. Development assistance was provided by the Canadian Department of National Defence, as the system is expected to have military as well as commercial applications. The sonar was presented in the spring of 1991 at a trade show.

Sport

LACROSSE

First played by the Algonquian Indian tribes of the St. Lawrence Valley in Canada, lacrosse is often considered to be Canada's national sport, but no game has ever been officially designated by this title. Lacrosse is the oldest organized sport in North America, and some form of it was played by fifty different first peoples across North America in the 1600s. The first peoples called it *baggataway*, and considered it not merely a game but also as a religious rite and physical training for warriors as well. Matches sometimes lasted for two to three days and involved fields five hundred yards long (four hundred fifty-seven meters) with teams ranging in size from twenty-five to two hundred men.

The name "lacrosse" was bestowed upon the game in 1636 by a Jesuit missionary who was reminded, by the stick used in the game, of a bishop's crozier or "crosse." In 1860, Montreal dental surgeon William George Beers, the father of modern lacrosse, set out standard rules for the game and two years later he published a book called *Lacrosse: The National Game of Canada*. The game spread quickly to the United States and Britain after 1867, when Beers organized the National Lacrosse Association. A Canadian touring team organized by Beers visited Britain in 1876, further promoting the game.

Women's lacrosse began in 1886 and has somewhat different rules than the men's game. There are no marked boundaries and the game is more fluid than men's lacrosse. In Edmonton, Alberta, at the 1978 Commonwealth Games, Canada, as host country, introduced lacrosse to the competition as the new sport. Appropriately, the vast majority of wooden lacrosse sticks are still made in North America by native peoples, although sticks made of plastic/aluminum are becoming more popular, especially in field lacrosse. One of the world's largest wooden lacrosse stick factories is located near Cornwall, Ontario, at the St. Regis Reserve. There is a Lacrosse Hall of Fame at New Westminster, British Columbia.

F IRST CURLING CLUB IN NORTH AMERICA

The game of curling was played informally in Canada before 1800, but it was not established in the country until 1807, when a group of Scottish immigrants formed the Montreal Curling Club, the first sports club in Canada and the first curling club in North America. This began a long, successful history of curling in Canada, facilitated by the abundance of lakes and rivers, long cold winters and plenty of safe ice on which to play. The participation of Scottish immigrants has also been an important part of the development of the game in Canada.

Curling clubs formed in Kingston (1820), Quebec (1821) and Halifax (1824) and in 1835 inter-city matches began. By 1839, locally-made stones of granite were being sold in Toronto for eight dollars a pair and in 1840, James Bicket's *The Canadian Curler's Manual* was published as the first book on curling in Canada. By 1858, the game had developed to the point that interprovincial matches took place. In 1865, the first international "bonspiel" was held in Buffalo between American and Canadian clubs. The first women's club formed in Montreal in 1894.

In 1902-03, the first Scottish team toured Canada giving widespread exposure to the sport. The team, captained by Reverend Mr. Kerr, played eleven matches against Canadian clubs and lost more than they won. They returned to Scotland very impressed by the growth and expertise of the game in Canada. When a Canadian team first toured Scotland in 1908, they won twenty-three of twenty-six matches, including three international contests for the Strathcona Cup.

Winnipeg became the center for curling in Canada by 1911. The Air Canada Silver Broom was established as the world curling championship in 1968 and Canada proceeded to win the first five competitions. The Canadian teams have been competitive ever since.

QUEEN'S PLATE—Oldest Continuously Run Turf Stakes Event in North America

On June 27, 1860, the Queen's Plate was first held at Toronto's Carleton Track. It is the oldest continuously run turf stakes event in North America, predating the Kentucky Derby by fifteen years. The race was set up in 1859, when Queen Victoria arranged for fifty guineas to be given to the winner of a horse race to be held annually somewhere in what is now Ontario. For the first four years the race was held in Toronto. It then moved to various towns in the province until 1883, when, with the Queen's approval, it returned to Toronto. It has been held there ever since and remains one of the most popular horse races in North America.

From 1902 to 1952 the race was called the King's Plate, since the reigning monarch is the event's official patron. In 1918 and 1919, World War I threatened the perpetuity of the race, so the fifty-ninth and sixtieth runnings were held as features of the Red Cross Horse Show in Toronto, the only races held in those two years. Since 1956, it has been run each June at the New Woodbine Racetrack in Toronto. The distance of the race was fixed at one and a quarter miles in 1957. In 1959, Elizabeth II and Prince Phillip attended the one-hundredth running of the race. The winner now receives the Queen's personal gift of fifty gold sovereigns (guineas are no longer minted) and a gold cup.

ICE HOCKEY

Although the antecedents of ice hockey are probably a mixture of European Shanty or Bandy games and a North American native peoples' form of ice hockey, the game as it is played today originated in Canada. There is some dispute as to when and where the first game of hockey was played. Some historians believe that the game was invented by men garrisoned at Halifax in 1853. However, the first recorded game took place on Christmas Day, 1855, in Kingston, Ontario, when members of the Royal Canadian Rifles stationed there cleared snow from an expanse of ice in the harbor, tied blades to their boots, and played with borrowed field hockey sticks and a lacrosse ball, following field hockey rules. The International Hockey Hall of Fame is quite properly located in Kingston.

There was little inter-area play until a group of students at McGill University in Montreal proposed a set of rules in 1875. The first public exhibition of the game was held on March 3, 1875, at Montreal's Victoria Skating Rink. The game caught on quickly after that, and by 1893, there were almost one hundred clubs in the Montreal area alone and the game was developing in the United States. That same year, Lord Stanley of Preston, Canada's governor general, was returning to England. He and his eight sons had become players and fans of hockey while in Canada and before he left, he spent ten guineas to donate the sterling bowl that now bears his name as the challenge cup for hockey. The Stanley Cup is the oldest trophy for which professional athletes compete in North America. It was first awarded to the Montreal Athletic Association, an amateur hockey team, on February 23, 1893, by Stanley himself. Up to 1912, only amateur teams competed for the trophy. In 1917, the professional National Hockey League (NHL) was formed in Montreal, and the trophy is now symbolic of the championship of the NHL.

A contributor to the development of hockey was John Forbes, of Dartmouth, Nova Scotia, who invented the spring skate in 1854, just as the game was beginning. Unlike previous skates, the spring skate could be firmly attached to a boot without means of straps or buckles but by means of a clamp that could be made to fit any foot size simply by adjusting a spring mechanism. Because the skate was so much easier to use, it led to the popularity of the sport and ultimately to the construction of covered rinks.

FIRST GOLF CLUB IN NORTH AMERICA

As with the first curling club in North America, Scottish immigrants were also responsible for the beginnings of golf in North America. In 1873, Scotsmen Alexander Dennistoun and John G. and David D. Sidey founded the Montreal Golf Club, the first golf club in

North America. Clubs sprang up in Quebec (1874), Toronto (1876), and Brantford (1879) soon afterwards. In 1884, Queen Victoria bestowed the "Royal" onto the name of the Montreal club, and it became the Royal Montreal Golf Club. Canada's premier golfer at the time, George Seymour Lyon (1858-1938), won the Canadian amateur title eight times between 1898 and 1914. In 1904, at the St. Louis Olympics, Lyon won the only Olympic gold medal ever awarded in golf.

FOOTBALL

It may surprise many people to hear that Canada affected modern football as it is played in the United States in two major ways. First, in 1874, a football team from McGill University visited Harvard to play two exhibition games. Though McGill lost both games, together with Harvard they set a precedent that affected all subsequent play of football in the United States. McGill arrived at Harvard one man short of the usual twelve-man team so the Harvard team fielded only eleven players to keep the game even. Since that time, the American game has been played with eleven players. The McGill team also played a style of the game that combined rugby and soccer, while Harvard played a version of soccer. Harvard took the hybrid style from McGill and spread it among Ivy League Colleges. The Canadian game is still played with twelve players; the first standard professional game with twelve players in Canada was played in 1921.

Slingshot football goalpost invented in Canada

The second change in the game came about through the efforts of Jim Trimble (born in 1918), a native of McKeesport, Pennsylvania, when he was the coach of the Montreal Alouettes, a Canadian Football League team. Trimble had finished the 1965 football season as coach of the Alouettes, and after three years with the team, he thought he was going to be fired. He also worked as a commentator for a Canadian radio/television company, and was sent to cover a British Columbia Lions game in Vancouver late in the 1965 season. Trimble knew the coach of the Lions, Dave Scrine, from his days as coach of the Philadelphia Eagles, and was very sympathetic to Scrine's misfortune with the team during the season. During the game, the Lions all-star receiver went for a long pass and, looking over his shoulder to catch the ball as he entered the end zone, he ran into the goalpost, dropped the ball and was injured and lost for the rest of the season. Scrine was fired the next day, and as Trimble flew back to Montreal he thought about what had happened to the receiver and how it could have been prevented.

He had made a few sketches of an idea for a different type of goalpost while on the plane, and he took them to Cedric Marsh, an engineer in Hudson, Quebec, working for Alcan, a Canadian aluminum company, to see if his idea could be constructed. His basic design became, with Marsh's engineering help, the revolutionary single base "slingshot" football goalpost.

Trimble's reasons for designing the goalposts were for safety—the single base was less of an obstacle to the players around the end zone—to reduce the interference of the goalposts in goal-line stands, and for aesthetics. He had to donate the first pair to the Montreal stadium in 1966 to get them to install them. But he had an easier time in the United States when the first pair were installed in the Orange Bowl in Miami for the Runner-Up Bowl game (played at the time between the runners-up in each National Football League (NFL) division) between the Philadelphia Eagles and the Dallas Cowboys.

The television coverage of the game boosted the goalpost's notoriety greatly. An added bonus was strong support from the officials in the game, who liked the single base, set six feet back from the goal line, because it did not obstruct their view of the plane of the goal line, which they have to watch to see if the ball crosses over it, scoring a touchdown.

The NFL was obsessed with the slingshot goalposts, and at its annual meeting in 1967 the posts were unanimously approved for use in the league. Trimble had more trouble in the U.S. Patent Office in Washington, D.C., when he applied for a patent in 1966. The application was at first rejected because it was considered a violation of the patent on the design of a curved lamp post. However, Trimble appealed the decision and was successful, based on the safety considerations of his design.

BASKETBALL

Basketball is now most popular as a men's game in the United States but it was invented by a Canadian and a women's team helped make it famous. Dr. James A. Naismith (1861-1939), of Almonte, Ontario, a graduate of McGill, while physical director of the International YMCA Training School in Springfield, Massachusetts, was asked to design a game that would "relieve the tedium of traditional gymnastics work" and calisthenics. It was agreed that the game should be flexible and avoid rough play, and Naismith's thirteen original rules were designed to enforce these aims: No contact was allowed, and running with the ball was prohibited. The rules were simple, the equipment wasn't extensive, and the play was adaptable to night and day and almost any age of player. The baskets were placed above the head so the ball had to be skillfully thrown in an arc to score, and speed and finesse rather than force were the main requirements. It was an ideal indoor team sport.

The first game was played in January 1892 in Springfield, and it was first introduced to Canada in Montreal by a graduate of Dr. Naismith's 1891 class. Originally, half bushel peach baskets (hence the name, basketball) were nailed to the railing of a balcony surrounding the gymnasium, but spectators interfered with the play; so backboards were designed. In 1900, an iron ring and bottomless net replaced the baskets.

Canada's most famous and successful basketball team was the Edmonton Commercial Grads, a team of women who continued to be coached by J. Percy Page after they finished high school in 1915. Until 1940, when they disbanded, the team won 502 out of 522 games and were Canadian champions nineteen times, and held the World Championship title for sixteen consecutive years. They competed in four Olympic demonstration matches, winning twenty-seven consecutive games, but received no medals because women's basketball was not an official Olympic sport until 1976. Thirty-eight women played with the Grads over their twenty-five year dynasty.

N ED HANLAN—Canada's World Champion Rower

He was the first Canadian athlete to gain international recognition and Canada's first world champion. He earned both distinctions through his stunning career as a rower. Edward "Ned" Hanlan (1855-1908) proved himself to be Ontario's best sculler between 1873 and 1876 by winning a series of races during that time. Over the next ten years he continued to dominate, competing in three hundred races and losing only six, establishing himself as the premier rower in the world. He won the Canadian championship in 1877 at Toronto and the U.S. championship in 1879 on the Allegheny River. In a race in England in May 1879, Hanlan beat the English champion by an incredible eleven lengths. On November 15, 1880, Hanlan challenged Australian Edward Trickett's claim to the world title, based on Trickett's defeat of the best British rower. He easily beat Trickett by three lengths over the four-and-a-quarter-mile course on the River Thames. The race attracted more than a hundred thousand spectators and wagers totalling five hundred thousand dollars were bet on both rowers. In 1884, Hanlan lost his world title to Australian William Beach, though he continued to row and race through the 1890s.

F IVE-PIN BOWLING

The game of five-pin bowling was invented by Thomas E. Ryan (1872-1961), a native of Guelph, Ontario. Ryan was raised in Toronto and was a noted baseball player and later a racehorse owner. In 1908-09, he was operating a ten-pin bowling alley in Toronto when he thought of a way to make the game more attractive to a larger group of players. He diminished the size and weight of the bowling ball, eliminating the need for finger holes, and reduced the size and number of pins from ten to five, simplifying the scoring.

After trying a number of experiments, Ryan had his father shave down five pins on a lathe, and Ryan placed the five pins on the ten-pin lane. He introduced the use of the duckpin ball and introduced a scoring system with the pins numbered one to five. Each player was allowed three balls per turn, with three turns per frame and ten frames per game. The maximum score was four hundred and fifty points. Ryan added an extra challenge by making it obligatory for the player to knock down the left corner (four) pin before they could be awarded any points. Because the pins were lighter, they flew through the air when the ball hit them, making the game far noisier than the ten-pin game. Ryan searched for a solution, and eventually added a thick rubber band (still used today) to the belly of the pin.

The game was an immediate success and soon became one of the most popular sports in Canada and the northern United States, although Ryan did not profit from it as he had not patented his invention. But he is recognized as the father of the game wherever it is played. Today more than one million Canadians play the game in over seven hundred centers across the country.

SYNCHRONIZED SWIMMING

Imagine that you're sinking underwater for the third and last time when suddenly you hear music. Swimmers head toward you performing calibrated water dances. Farfetched? Not really! The basics of synchronized swimming originated in the strokes and figures in the Canadian Royal Life Saving Society program. The performance of a series of movements in water, coordinated with music, provided a competitive outlet for young women who were not attracted to speed swimming.

The first competition took place at the Y.M.C.A. in Montreal (the first in North America), in 1923. The Canadian Amateur Swimming Association drew up formal rules in 1924, and that year the Province of Quebec held the first provincial championship in "ornamental" or "scientific" swimming. Not until the 1940s was it called "synchronized swimming."

In the figures section of the competition, each swimmer performs a series of six figures for the judges. If they are part of a duet or team, the swimmers' individual scores are averaged together to get one score. This score is combined with their duet or team score in the routine section of the competition, in which the swimmers perform synchronized routines to music. The divisions of solo and duet synchronized swimming were included in the competitions for the first time in the 1984 Olympics.

Recognized as the leaders in synchronized swimming, Canadian swimmers have consistently won the medals. Since 1984,

Carolyn Waldo has won the gold six times in the solo event, and, with her partner, Michelle Cameron, the gold in the duet event seven times. At the FINA (Federation International de Nacion Aquatique) World Cup in 1985 at Indianapolis, the equivalent of the world championship in other sports, Canadian swimmers won the solo, duet and team competitions. Only the top eight teams in the world compete in this event.

In 1986, at the World Aquatic Championships in Madrid, Spain and at the Commonwealth Games in Edinburgh, Scotland, Canadian swimmers again won the solo, duet and team competitions. In Madrid, Waldo became the first synchronized swimmer to be awarded a perfect score of ten.

In 1987, Canadian swimmers won all three events at the Pan-Pacific Championships at Tokyo, Japan, and the solo and duet events at the FINA World Cup in Egypt, where the U.S. team won the team event. In all of these events, Waldo won the solo and, with Cameron, the duet competition. Also in 1987, Carolyn Waldo was named Canada's female athlete of the year and awarded the Bobby Rosenfeld Award (named after Canada's female athlete of the half-century 1900-50) by Canadian Press and its affiliate Broadcast News.

At the 1988 Summer Olympics in Seoul, Korea, Waldo won the gold in the solo event, and, with Cameron, the gold in the duet competition. After the Olympics both retired, ending their streak of victories. Waldo had not been beaten in the solo event since she won the silver medal at the 1984 Olympics. Born in Beaconsfield, Quebec, she moved to Calgary, Alberta, in 1984 to train with Cameron.

Since Waldo's and Cameron's retirement, Canadian swimmers, notably Sylvia Frechette, Natalie Guay, Andrea Manning, Nancy Bélanger, Cari Read and Marie José Laviolette, continued to excel in international competitions.

F IRSTS AND FOREMOSTS IN FIGURE SKATING

Barbara Ann Scott - First North American to win Olympic crown and world championship in figure skating

In a brief two years, Canadian Barbara Ann Scott had an immense impact on women's figure skating worldwide, setting a precedent in competitive skating that changed the face of the sport forever. In her routines in competition, Scott's athletic style, including spins, turns and jumps that had never been executed by a woman on ice before, forever relegated to the past the graceful gliding that had marked Norwegian Sonja Henie's skating in the early days of the sport.

Scott became Canada's national junior champion in 1940, and in 1944 she won the national senior title, holding that position through 1948. But in 1947, Scott stunned the sports world at the World Championships in Stockholm, executing three double loop jumps to finish her free- skate routine, and scoring two perfect 6.0 marks on her way to becoming the first North American world champion. The next year, at the St. Moritz Winter Olympics, Scott defended her title as world champion and scored another first as she became the first North American to win the Olympic gold in figure skating. Back in Canada, Scott was showered with adulation for her accomplishments, including being named Canada's outstanding athlete in 1945, 1947, and 1948. She was also eventually made a member of the Canadian Sports Hall of Fame. But perhaps the changes she affected in women's figure skating during those years represent her most lasting achievement.

Don Jackson—Seven 6.0s in a world competition

Donald Jackson of Oshawa, Ontario, earned an unprecedented seven 6.0s for his free-skating performance in the 1962 World Championship competition at Prague, Czechoslovakia. He began the final part of the competition forty-five points behind the home-town favorite,

Karol Divin, but skated a miraculous performance that included twenty-two jumps without a flaw and the first triple Lutz ever performed in competition. When the marks for artistic impression and technical merit were posted, he earned nine 5.9s, two 5.8s, and the seven 6.0s, enough to overtake Divin and win the gold medal.

Kurt Browning—First quadruple jump in competition

Born in 1966 in Caroline, Alberta, Kurt Browning learned to skate at age six on a backyard rink. Sixteen years later, on March 25, 1988, at the World Championships at Budapest, Hungary, Browning completed an unprecedented quadruple toe loop during his long program free skate. Taking off on his left toe, he revolved four times in the air and landed on his right foot. Though he followed Canadians Don Jackson and Vern Taylor (who in 1976 was the first to do a triple axel in competition) into the history books with his feat, Browning only placed sixth in the 1988 World Championships. However, in 1989 in Paris, and 1990 in Halifax, Nova Scotia, Browning won the World Championship, becoming the first Canadian male skater to win back-to-back world titles. Though he had difficulties landing certain jumps during the 1989-90 season and didn't complete the quadruple jump, his performance in the 1990 competition was still good enough to top Soviet skater Viktor Petrenko. In 1990, Browning was named Canada's male athlete of the year and awarded the Lionel Conacher Award (named after Canada's male athlete of the half-century 1900-50) by Canadian Press and its affiliate Broadcast News.

MARILYN BELL AND CINDY NICHOLAS

As the first person to swim across Lake Ontario and the youngest person to ever swim the English Channel, Marilyn Bell (born in 1937) of Canada is a national legend. She entered the Lake Ontario swim unofficially at the age of sixteen, along with another Torontonian, Winnie Roach Leuzler, age twenty-eight. They swam alongside Florence Chadwick of the United States, who had been invited to swim the lake by the Toronto's Canadian National Exhibition (CNE) as part of their traditional endurance exhibition. Chadwick was known as the best long distance swimmer in the world at the time and was to receive ten thousand dollars for the feat. In contrast, Bell was virtually unknown, although she had received some publicity for being the first woman to finish a twenty-five mile (forty kilometer) swim in Atlantic City eight weeks earlier. She entered the lake swim with Leuzler to prove that Canadian swimmers could also complete the feat. The *Toronto Star* paid for their expenses.

On September 19, 1954, the swimmers entered the water at Youngstown, New York, a little before midnight. Not known for her speed but rather for her endurance and stamina, Bell did not expect to win the race, but by noon the next day she was the only one left in the water. Radio and newspaper reporters seized upon the drama of the situation, and when Bell reached the shores of the exhibition grounds twenty hours and fifty-nine minutes later an estimated hundred thousand people were there to greet her. She had swum a forty-mile (65 kilometer) zig-zag route to cover the thirty-two-mile (51.5 kilometer) distance across the lake and was awarded the ten thousand dollar prize. When asked why she had done it, Bell exclaimed: "I did it for Canada!"

In 1955, on her second try, Bell swam the English Channel from France to England in fourteen and a half hours. In both 1954 and 1955, Bell was named Canada's Woman of the Year for her accomplishments. In 1956, on her second try, she became the first woman to swim the Straits of Juan de Fuca (between Vancouver Island in Canada and the Olympic Peninsula of the State of Washington), covering the distance of one hundred miles (one hundred sixty-one kilometers) in ten and a half hours.

Cindy Nicholas, meanwhile, made her own mark on the English Channel when she completed the first double crossing of the Channel by a woman on September 8, 1977. Not only did she complete her nonstop swim, she lowered the record for a double crossing, previously held by American Jon Erikson, by ten hours and five minutes. That feat gained her the title of Canada's female athlete of the year for 1977. However, she was not able to set the England-to-France record during the swim, and on the way back fell short of her record for the France-to-England part of the swim. In 1981, Nicholas attempted an unprecedented triple crossing of the Channel, but completed only two crossings before being forced to stop by bad weather. A few days later, Erikson completed the first triple-crossing of the Channel.

L ASER SAILBOAT

A telephone doodle, a "Thank God It's Friday" attitude, and a retail request for an economic family sailboat brought fame and fortune to three Canadians. The world's most popular sailboat, the Laser, was first designed and produced by Bruce Kirby, Ian Bruce and Hans Fogh in 1969. Bruce Kirby went on from designing the Laser for the "America's Tea Cup" regatta in Wisconsin to designing Canada's entries in the America's Cup. But that early design for a twelve foot-long (3.66 meters) fiberglass dinghy, now known and loved worldwide, was initially turned down for production by the retailer.

Despite its humble beginnings, the Laser made sailing accessible to many more people of all ages than ever before. The simplicity yet high performance of the design, the boat's relatively low cost ($2,395 U.S. and $3,099 Canadian in 1991), the standard-ized form that allowed international competition, and the boat's transportability are all factors in the popularity of the Laser. In 1987, eighteen years after its initial design, 139,000 Lasers had been built worldwide, and there were 18,000 registered members of the International Laser Class Association, the second-largest and fastest-growing sailing class in the world . The Laser is sailed in over fifty countries and produced around the world by licensees of a holding company. The boat's original manufacturer, Performance Sailcraft of Quebec, went into receivership in January 1983. The license for North America and the Caribbean is held by Pearson Yachts of Rhode Island which took it over from Laser International, the successor of Performance Sailcraft. Other manufacturers are involved in England, Europe, Japan, Australia, and New Zealand.

The boat was first conceived by Kirby, then editor of the magazine *One Design and Offshore Yachtsman* in Stamford, Connecticut. During a telephone conversation with Ian Bruce, an engineer in Montreal, who had been been asked to develop camping equipment for a large Canadian retailer, including possibly a family sailboat, Kirby sketched a boat similar to what the Laser finally became. Now dubbed "the Million Dollar Doodle", it hangs in Kirby's office in Rowayton, Connecticut, complete with his small daughter's attempt to spell 'spinnaker' in one corner. By mid-October 1969, Kirby had completed the basic design of what he first called the "Weekender," and had sent the drawings off to Ian Bruce.

However, the retailer decided not to produce the boat, and the design might have been shelved forever if Kirby and Bruce had not decided to build a model of the boat for a regatta held by Kirby's magazine in 1970. Called "America's Tea Cup," the regatta was held in Wisconsin, and only boats that cost less than a thousand dollars were allowed to enter. Kirby and Bruce built the boat themselves and recruited Hans Fogh, an Olympic sailor who had emigrated from Denmark to Canada in 1969, to design the sail and skipper the boat in the regatta. To go along with the "weekender" idea, Fogh stitched the letters T.G.I.F., for "Thank God it's Friday," on the sail. In its first race the boat placed second in its class, and that night Fogh recut the sail, making the boat perform even better in subsequent races.

Dick Tillman, an American, set the standard for Laser form and technique in the 1970s while winning three consecutive North American championships. In 1982, Canadian Laser sailors were considered to be at the top of the class. Terry Neilson and Andy Roy, both Canadians, proved this to be true by placing first and second in the world championships in Italy. Neilson went onto skipper *Canada II*, Canada's entry in the 1986 America's Cup.

The Laser is typically Canadian in that it has given pleasure to many people all over the world, while its creators have maintained a relatively low profile.

ONLY SPORT DATA BASE IN THE WORLD

Before 1973, no resource existed that gave a systematic reference for information about sport and exercise, not even a general bibliography, let alone a complete database. Since that time, people have become more aware that regular exercise can help increase life expectancy and improve general physical and mental conditions, and coaching and sports medicine have developed greatly. In response, the Coaching Association of Canada (CAC) developed a system to make information about sport available to coaches, sport therapists, athletes, administrators, and the people who are attempting to put their awareness into practice.

The idea for a database came from the Canadian government's aim to develop a training program for coaches and its realization that it had to inform them first. Thus, an information center was needed. But, the requisite material and a means of accessing it were not available anywhere. The government "more or less blindly" supported a team for five years up to 1973, to develop the necessary database; it has not been unsatisfied with the results.

Established in 1973, SPORT Database has become an international information system, and twenty-five to thirty countries use it regularly. It is recognized by the International Association for Sport (IASI) and by the International Council for Sport Science and Physical Education (ICSSPE) as the International Database for Sport. The Database is located at the Sport Information Resource Center in the Canadian Sport and Fitness Administration Centre in Ottawa, Ontario. The United States is the most active subscriber, and Canada second. Also, twenty countries now participate in an exchange of material, including the United States, as well as the University of Oregon. Says Gilles Chiasson, the current president of SPORT Database, "I would like to see the Database controlled by its participants; then we could go back to the original mandate that the government gave us."

SPORT Database has also fulfilled a general purpose beyond being an information source just for coaches. It includes indexing from over twenty-two thousand books and two thousand sports-related journals, on topics including training, sports medicine, sports administration and sports law. It has contributed to the development of Canadian and international sport and has helped to emphasize the development of the physical condition of the general population of Canada.

COACHING

When little kids lose sight of how much fun baseball and hockey can be or teenagers are not able to compete in their sport in college because they were burned out and pushed too hard to win by their parents and coaches in high school, the coaching system needs to be examined. In order to prevent these cases, a basic change in the attitude toward sport is necessary. While people in the United States often look to the private sector to solve such a problem, Canadians more often look to their government to take the lead. In this case, the Canadian government came up with a solution that private companies in the United States are now adopting for profit.

In 1974, the Ontario government developed the National Coaching Development Program (now called the National Coaching Certification Program (NCCP)), to help ensure that coaches at all levels of competition are aware of the physical and psychological needs of the players and can communicate with parents, plan a practice, and teach skills. By 1982, the program had spread to all ten provinces and by 1985, 165,000 coaches had taken at least one course. It is aimed at producing coaches who will make players whole individuals as well as winning team members. The classes for coaches are divided into five levels, the first three of which are aimed at volunteer coaches. These emphasize the need to develop skills and sportsmanship through training in theory and technique and the importance of practical experience over winning at all costs. As one gymnastics coach explained, he had to teach a group of thirteen- and fourteen-year-old boys very difficult moves in order to win a competition, without being able to spend enough time on the basics. This inevitably means that the player will be less successful at a later age.

Hockey is an area of particular concern in Canada. One staff member of the Certification program said that many Canadian players are missing the fundamental skills of the game, a fact that reflects on inadequate coaching during their formative years. Judging by the similar programs developed by some U.S. companies after the Canadian system was instituted, the same development of coaching is needed in the United States. It can only be good for the sport and the individuals involved if the training received allows the players to develop and become more skillful and continue to play the game while not damaging their talents or physical capabilities.

STEVE PODBORSKI

On March 5, 1982, Canadian Steve Podborski (born in 1957) became the first non-European to win the World Cup downhill skiing championship. He won three consecutive World Cup downhills that year and in one, at Kitzbühel, Austria, his winning speed of one hundred miles per hour (one hundred and sixty-one kilometers per hour) was the fastest time ever recorded on the course.

Podborski was on skis at age of two and began racing when he was ten years old. Incredibly, Podborski joined the Canadian alpine ski team in 1973, when he was only sixteen. Over the next ten years he became a key member of the "Crazy Canucks" Canadian downhill ski team, winning eight World Cup races, the most successful Canadian racer to date. He won his first World Cup race in December 1979 at Morzine, France. At the 1980 Olympics at Lake Placid, New York, Podborski won the bronze medal in the downhill race. Between 1980 and 1984 he had more top-three finishes in World Cup races than any other racer in the world. At the end of the 1984 season, Podborski retired from the World Cup Circuit, the last of the five original "Crazy Canucks" to do so.

The Crazy Canucks were a group of young ski racers from various parts of Canada who skied with such abandon it led French journalist and World Cup founder Serge Lang to label them with the name. However, he spelled it "Cannucks" and that is how its is always printed in Europe. Between December 1975 and January 1984, Canucks Jim Hunter, Dave Irwin, Dave Murray, Ken Read, and Podborski won fourteen World Cup downhills in Europe, including four consecutive victories on the toughest course on the circuit, the Hahnekamm at Kitzbühel.

FIRST NORTH AMERICAN TEAM TO WIN WORLD CUP BOBSLEDDING CHAMPIONSHIP

At the last race of the 1989-90 World Cup bobsledding season in Calgary, Canada's four-man bobsledding team was on the verge of winning the overall title. Chris Lori, driver for the Canada I bobsled, and teammates Ken LeBlanc, John Graham, and Doug Currier had placed first in the heats, just three-tenths of a second ahead of the Canada II sled, driven by Greg Haydenluck. The Canada I team had placed nineteenth, eighteenth, sixth, eighth, and second in the first five races of the season and needed a first place finish in the final race to win the championship. Five out of the six races count towards the overall title for the four-man bobsled.

When the race came to a close on Sunday, March 11, 1990, the Canada I team had won the race and the title, edging out the team led by Maris Poikans of the Soviet Union by two points overall. Poikans had not travelled to Calgary for the final race as he already had five complete races to count towards the overall points race. The victory by Lori's sled was also the first time a Canadian team had won a World Cup bobsled race.

Twenty-six years earlier, on Thursday February 4, 1964, Canada's four-man bobsled team won one of the training runs at the Winter Olympics in Innsbruck, Austria. It was the first time Canada had entered a team in Olympic bobsled events. The team had taken shape over the previous ten years, slowly building up from a group of three young men—Lamont Gordon, Victor Emery, and John Emery, who went off on their own to try out sledding in Europe in the spring of 1955—then adding Charles Rathgeb and setting off to participate in the World Championships in 1959. The team grew in number to have two sleds at the World Championships from 1960 to 63, placing fourth in the four-man in 1962.

The 1964 Olympic competition began on February 5, and after two of the four runs the Canada I sled, driven by Vic Emery with teammates Doug Anakin, John Emery, and brakeman Peter Kirby, was in first place. One of their runs that day equalled the track record. The third and fourth runs were spread out over the next two days. On Saturday, February 6, the Canada I team had the second fastest run after Austria but remained in first place. The next day, officials decided that there should be a practice run before the final run. The Austrian team was in second place, and the local citizens were hoping for victory. Canada I was second in the practice run, but went on to win the final race and Canada's first and only gold medal of the 1964 Winter Olympics, an amazing upset over the vastly more experienced European teams.

Selected Bibliography

Badash, Lawrence. *Dictionary of Scientific Biography*. Vol. 3. New York: Charles Scribner's Sons, 1975.

Baka, R., G. Redmond and B. Schrodt. *Sport Canadiana*. Edmonton: Executive Sport Publications Ltd., 1980.

Bannerman, Joan. *Leading Ladies: Canada*. Belleville, Ontario: Mike Publishing Co., 1967.

Bean, Gladys, ed. *The History of Synchronized Swimming in Canada*. Ottawa: Canadian Amateur Synchronized Swimming Association, 1985.

Bearden, Jim and Linda Jean Butler. *Shadd: The Life and Times of Mary Shadd Cary*. Toronto: NC Press Ltd, 1977.

Bochner, Sally. *All About Us*. Toronto: National Film Board, no date.

Brown, J.J. *Ideas in Exile: A History of Canadian Invention*. Toronto: McClelland and Stewart, 1967.

The Canadian Encyclopedia. Vols. 1-3. Edmonton: Hurtig Publishers, 1985.

Canadian Centennial Library. *Great Canadians*. Toronto: Canadian Centennial Library, 1965.

Colombo, John Robert. *Colombo's Canadian References*. Toronto: Oxford University Press, 1976.

_____. *1001 Questions About Canada*. Toronto: Doubleday Canada Ltd., 1986.

Cudden, J.A. *The MacMillan Dictionary of Sports and Games*. New York: MacMillan Press, 1980.

Encyclopedia Canadiana. Toronto: Grolier of Canada, 1977.

Filion, John ed. *The Canadian World Almanac & Book of Facts.* Agincourt, Ontario: Global Press,1989.

Grosvenor House Press. *Winners: A Century of Canadian Sport.* Toronto: Grosvenor House Press, 1985.

The Guinness Book of Records. Guinness Publishing, 1988.

Guvia, Francine and Helen Lewis. *Blacks in Canada: In Search of the Promise.* Edmonton: Harambee Centres, Canada, 1988.

Haber, Louis. *Black Pioneers of Science and Invention.* New York: Harcourt, Brace & World, 1970.

Hancock, Dr. Trevor "Beyond Health Care." *The Futurist* (August 1982) 4-13.

_____ . "Beyond Health Care: From Public Health Policy to Healthy Public Policy." *Canadian Journal of Public Health* 76, sup. 1 (May/June 1985) 9-10.

Hill, Daniel G. *The Freedom Seekers: Blacks in Early Canada.* Agincourt, Ontario: The Book Society of Canada, 1981.

Information Canada. *The Mirrored Spectrum: A Collection of Reports for the Non-scientist and Non-engineer about Achievements in Canadian Technology.* Vol. 1. Toronto: Information Canada, 1973.

Kohr, Dr. John R. *A Selection of Canadian Achievements in Science and Technology, 1800-1964.* Ottawa: National Research Council of Canada, 1964.

Leach, Nathanial. *Reaching Out to Freedom: The Second Baptist Connection* (revised edition eyewitness history). Detroit: Second Baptist Church, 1988.

Makow, Henry and H.T. Stevinson. "C.P.I.—A Crash Position Indicator for Aircraft", *I.R.E. Transactions on Aeronautical and Navigational Electronics.* September, 1959.

McKay, Paul. *Electric Empire: The Inside Story of Ontario Hydro.* Toronto: Between the Lines, Ontario, 1983.

Miller, J.R. *Skyscrapers Hide the Heavens: A History of Indian-White Relations in Canada.* Toronto: University of Toronto Press, 1989.

Moody, J. and Gilbert C. Fite, *The Credit Union Movement: Origins and Development 1850-1970.* Lincoln: University of Nebraska Press, 1971.

Myers, Jay. *The Fitzhenry and Whiteside Book of Canadian Facts and*

Dates. Markham, Ontario: Fitzhenry and Whiteside, 1986.

National Film Board. *Colin Low*. Toronto: National Film Board, no date.

Nostbakken, Janis and Jack Humphrey. *The Canadian Inventions Book: Innovations, discoveries and firsts*. Toronto: Greey de Pencier Publications, 1976.

Ondaatje, Christopher and Gordon Currie. *Olympic Victory: The Story Behind the Canadian Bob-Sled Club's Incredible Victory at the 1964 Winter Olympic Games*. Toronto: Pagurian Press Ltd., 1967.

Outreach. *One Thousand and One Reasons For Being Proud to be a Canadian*. Toronto: Outreach, 1974.

Porter, Tom "The Constitution of the Six Nations." In *Pathways to Self-Determination: Canadian Indians and the Canadian State*. Edited by Leroy Little Bear et al. Toronto: University of Toronto Press, 1984.

Prentice, Alison et al. *Canadian Women: A History*. Toronto: Harcourt Brace Jovanovich, 1988.

Quick Canadian Facts. *Quick Canadian Facts*. 31st edition. Toronto: Quick Canadian Facts, 1976.

Robertson, Patrick. *The Book of Firsts*. New York: Clarkson N. Pooter, 1974.

Russell, Paul and Robert Jeffrey. *Trivia: Inconsequential but Irresistible Facts About Canada*. Toronto: Gage Publishing, 1980.

Sammons, Vivian Ovelton. *Blacks in Science and Medicine*. New York: Hemisphere Publishing, 1990.

Tillman, Dick and Dave Fowlison. *The New Laser Sailing*. Boston: SAIL Books, 1983.

Van Sertima, Ivan, ed. *Blacks in Science: ancient and modern*. New Brunswick, NJ: Transaction Books, 1984.

Wasson, Tyler, ed. *Nobel Prize Winners: An H.W. Wilson Biographical Dictionary*. New York: H.W. Wilson, 1987.

Wise, S.F. and Douglas Fisher, *Canada's Sporting Heroes*. Don Mills, Ontario: General Publishing, 1974.

Duff Conacher, a Canadian,
is a graduate of the University of
Toronto Faculty of Law.

Nadia Milleron, an American,
is a graduate of Smith College and
presently a student at the
University of Iowa School of Law.